LEADS & CONCLUSIONS

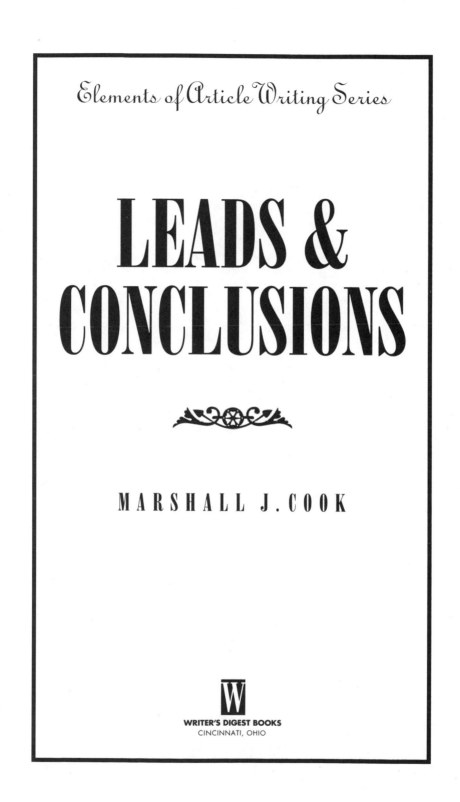

Elements of Article Writing Series

LEADS & CONCLUSIONS

MARSHALL J. COOK

WRITER'S DIGEST BOOKS
CINCINNATI, OHIO

Leads and Conclusions. Copyright © 1995 by Marshall J. Cook. Printed and bound in the United States of America. All rights reserved. No part of this book may be reproduced in any form or by any electronic or mechanical means including information storage and retrieval systems without permission in writing from the publisher, except by a reviewer, who may quote brief passages in a review. Published by Writer's Digest Books, an imprint of F&W Publications, Inc., 1507 Dana Avenue, Cincinnati, Ohio, 45207. 1-800-289-0963. First edition.

This hardcover edition of *Leads and Conclusions* features a "self-jacket" that eliminates the need for a separate dust jacket. It provides sturdy protection for your book while it saves paper, trees and energy.

99   98   97   96   95   5   4   3   2   1

Library of Congress Cataloging in Publication Data

Cook, Marshall
    Leads and conclusions / by Marshall J. Cook.
        p.   cm. — (Elements of article writing)
    Includes index.
    ISBN 0-89879-661-X
    1. Authorship. I. Title. II. Series.
PN147.C773   1995
808'.02—dc20   94-23650
                                                                        CIP

Edited by Catherine M. Brohaugh
Designed by Brian Roeth
Cover Design by Sandy Conopeotis

ABOUT THE AUTHOR

Marshall J. Cook is a professor at the University of Wisconsin-Madison Outreach, where he teaches workshops on creativity, writing and publishing.

He edits *Creativity Connection*, a quarterly newsletter for writers.

He wrote and self-published *Writing for the Joy of It* (Will Beymer Press, 1990). He has authored *Freeing Your Creativity: A Writer's Guide* and *How to Write With the Skill of a Master and the Genius of a Child* (both for Writer's Digest Books), and *Hometown Wisconsin* (Savage Press).

He has published a couple of hundred magazine articles and short stories in publications ranging from *Law and Order* to *Working Mother*. He has also written several novels, and is working on another, *The Year of the Buffalo*.

He is married to the former Ellen Malloy, and they have one son, Jeremiah; Rosie, the rogue miniature Schnauzer; and two nearly noseless Persian cats, Ralph and Norton.

To Ellen Malloy Cook and Jeremiah Patrick Cook, who fill my life with promising leads and satisfying conclusions.

ACKNOWLEDGMENTS

Everybody I've ever read and everybody I've ever interviewed has been my teacher.

My college mentor, Bill Rivers, taught me the power of "language in its shirt sleeves."

Clarke Stallworth used to be a "copy fixer" and became a nurturing editor. He taught me to "keep the get high and the cost low."

My colleague and friend, Blake Kellogg, daily teaches me to respect clean, clear writing and honors me by asking for advice from his junior partner.

With her dedication and unfailing enthusiasm, another colleague and friend, Chris DeSmet, keeps reminding me why we write.

My writing partner, Dorothy Durning Malloy, talks with me about the things that matter so much to both of us, words in print and the glories they offer us.

George Cook taught me to give my best effort to any task I took on and to work with honesty and integrity. I've never had a better teacher or a more important lesson.

TABLE OF CONTENTS

INTRODUCTION

Don't even think of her as a reader. Not yet.

As she turns the pages of a magazine, glancing at a headline here, a photo caption there, pausing to read the first few sentences of an article, she's a browser, a scanner, a grazer. She hasn't yet made the commitment to become a reader.

In the words of the old Hank Williams song, she's just "window shoppin'."

A magazine or a shelf full of books is a little like a shopping mall. The shopper may enter the mall with one purchase in mind. She certainly has no intention of entering all those other stores, and no time to do so even if she wanted to. But she's willing to glance at the windows of the other stores, in case something might interest her. If she's not in too much of a hurry, she may be hoping a display will catch her attention and invite her in. If she's in a big rush, which is probable most of the time, she may regard the window, no matter how enticing, as more obstacle than opportunity.

In the same way, she doesn't plan to read every word of a magazine or select every book in the store or library. Magazine articles and books must compete for attention, just like the stores in a mall. Illustrations and color may attract attention, but those first few words of text—headlines, chapter headings and leads for your nonfiction articles or book chapters—are the real attraction. A huge SALE! 70% OFF sign in the window won't bring the browser into the store, after all, unless the item on display in the window is something she wants.

To entice that shopper into your store, or the reader into your article or book, you must offer something of genuine worth. And she must be able to see the value *immediately*. Folks don't study windows; they glance at them.

If you would turn a window shopper into a customer, a grazer into a reader, you must issue a compelling invitation in your lead, based on this powerful promise: *For your precious time, I will give you something of value.*

My friend Clarke Stallworth, former managing editor of the Birmingham, Alabama *News*, puts it this way: "There are only two things a reader wants to know—what do I get and how much is it going to cost me?" You've got to promise to keep the "get" relatively high and the "cost," in terms of time and energy required to read, relatively low.

Think of the promise to the reader this way: *The words that follow will in some way enhance your life.*

How can you enhance the reader's life? What can you offer her in exchange for her precious time? Here are some possibilities.

- *Usable information* — tips on how to be a better parent; how to get and stay physically, mentally and emotionally healthy; how to perform better on the job; how to make more money and protect the money she's got; sixteen fun one-day car trips she can take with her family; the seven warning signs that her teenager is using drugs.

- *Interesting information* — how the town she lives in got its name; who decides what books the library orders; the story behind the kindly old crossing guard who has shepherded three generations of kids to school — the sort of trivia that makes games like *Jeopardy* and *Trivial Pursuit* so popular, stories and facts that have no practical application but are nice to know.

- *Entertainment* — the great gift of laughter, the emotional release, the relief of setting her troubles aside, to be lifted out of herself and her world and into someone else's.

- *Inspiration* — an example to encourage and challenge her to be better than she thought she could be.

Think about the books and articles you've chosen to read lately. Why did you read them? Your reasons probably fall into one or more of these categories.

Notice the sort of words we've used so far to discuss this delicate task of converting a window shopper into a customer, a grazer into a reader: *entice, invitation, promise, offer*. Notice, too, that we haven't used words like *force, coerce, trick* or *trap*. You can't force the browser to become a reader. She doesn't have to read what you've written. You must earn her time and attention, which she must freely give.

You probably could trick her ("Extramarital sex is again running rampant in the suburbs! And so is the use of home computers."). But only once. When she catches on — and it won't take long — she'll not only stop reading, she'll remember who tricked her, so she can avoid stepping into a second trap.

You don't want to try to snare every passerby. There's not much use in luring a vegetarian into a meat market, unless, of course, you've put in a line of sprouts and grains. Your invitation should be reader-specific, attracting anyone potentially interested in your subject and the way you approach that subject, and allowing the others to pass you by.

You should be open, honest and honorable in your intentions toward your reader. You're asking her to trust you with one of the most precious things she has, her time. Never abuse that trust or take the reader for granted.

Respect your reader. Whether you're writing for *Baseball America* or *Bride's*, *Road & Track* or *Redbook*, for college graduates or grade school dropouts, you can safely make only two assumptions about that reader:

- she's as smart as you are, and
- she's as busy as you are, too.

So much work, so few words

Your lead, then, must issue a strong, honest invitation, a promise of benefit. To do so, it must announce the subject, introduce the focus, and establish the tone. *Subject* is what you're writing about, your topic. *Focus* is the slant or angle you've taken toward the subject. *Tone* is the emotional context—humorous, confrontational, satiric, informative, angry. "Housebreaking your puppy" is a subject. "Housebreaking your puppy in three easy steps" provides a slant (key word—"easy"). "How to housebreak your puppy without breaking up your house" suggests a light tone.

That's quite a burden to pile onto the lead, especially when you realize that you must accomplish all these tasks quickly. When that grazer glances at your lead, remember, she hasn't yet committed to being a reader. She simply wants to find out what you're offering, as quickly as possible, so she can decide whether to linger or move on. Your lead must work its magic in just a few words.

How few is "a few"?

Inflexible rules and formulas just don't work when we're dealing with a flesh-and-blood reader, with all her quirks and idiosyncrasies. I won't offer a magic number here. But I will share some conclusions from the Direct Mail Marketing Association, a group with a strong interest in discovering how many words a reader will tolerate.

They set out to find the "cliff," the point where folks stop reading their direct mail solicitations (denegrated as "junk mail" when we aren't interested in what they're selling). They discovered what any reader probably could have told them: We make the critical read/don't read decision almost immediately. Many never get past the envelope (even if it promises "You may have already won a billion dollars" or threatens dire personal consequences if you don't open it immediately). Of those who do open the envelope, virtually everybody who stops reading does so *within the first twenty-five words* of text. Get a reader past twenty-five words, and you'll probably keep her the rest of the way.

Just those few words/images in the window get the window shopper into the store or send her on her way. Once she has converted from a window shopper to a potential customer, she'll want lots of words—

specific information, answers to her questions, solutions to her problems.

Does this mean that all leads must be twenty-five words or less? It does not. The lead for a 750-word magazine short must get to the point a lot faster than the introduction to a 750-page book. Leads for columns, reminiscences and profiles are often more leisurely than those for how-to and other service pieces. Length may also depend on subject, slant, publication and audience.

But the twenty-five-word warning does mean that your first words *must* be interesting. If they aren't, nobody will ever see the rest.

Why some books get taken home

On one of my frequent forays to the bookstore (where I spend a great deal of my time and too much of my money), I was intrigued by the title of a book by Ron Powers, so I plucked the book off the shelf, opened to the first chapter, and read these words:

> Toward evening of a late-winter day, late in a dark decade in the fortunes of American city life, I rented a car at a small airport in western Kentucky and started driving on a two-lane highway toward Illinois.

Forty words in, and no hint of where we're going, much less why. But I already knew that the driver had a specific destination in mind and that he knew how to get there. That's a sure hand on the steering wheel. I read a little more.

> I was headed for a town—a violent and sorrowful little town that lay wedged between two rivers at the southern tip of the state, a place of cruel secrets and Gothic ruin, which bore the tragically hopeful name of Cairo.

I was pretty well hooked, not so much by the subject as by the slant and tone ("violent and sorrowful . . . cruel secrets . . . tragically hopeful"). The next sentence finished the job:

> Cairo was dying.

After just these first three paragraphs, I closed the book, took it to the cashier, paid my money, and took *Far From Home* to my home and read every word.

Talking your way through a lead

Only other writers care about the process the writer went through to create the writing. Denise Shekerjian gives us this sort of insight in her marvelous book, *Uncommon Genius: How Great Ideas Are Born.* She set out to discover the traits creative people have in common. She interviewed forty recipients of the MacArthur Foundation grants, the so-called "genius awards" — writers, scientists, theater instructors, even a clown, all uncommonly creative and diverse people.

She no doubt wanted to begin her book with a pithy observation that would somehow summarize all she had learned, somehow capture the essence of the mystery of creativity. That's a real load of bricks for the writer to try to hoist in the first few words — the sort of bricks we use to build writers' blocks.

Shekerjian bravely launched her first chapter, "Talent and the Long Haul," with this observation: "A conscious application of raw talent, far more than luck or accident, is at the core of every creative moment."

Subject — creativity. Slant — creativity is conscious and intentional. Tone — expository, serious but not stuffy.

But not the lead Shekerjian wanted. Instead of hitting the delete, she let the first attempt stand and allowed us to overhear her creative monologue. (The italics are hers):

> *No, no, that will never do. Even if it's true, it's not the kind of thing a reader wants to hear. It comes across as brutal and heartless. Most decent people are modest and tentative in their efforts. They suspect they have no special talent for anything. They fear they are ordinary.*
> *Better start over.*

So she did, asserting in her second take: "The cultivation of aptitude, far more than coincidence or inspiration, is responsible for most creative breakthroughs."

> *Hardly better.*
> *You're going to discourage readers with a line like that. What everyone wants is magic, a prescription a druggist can fill, the key to the secret rose garden where the flowers bloom forever. What they want is The Trick to creativity so that they will be assured of a richer, more satisfying life. Try again.*

Her third attempt was much more relaxed and conversational. "Identify your own peculiar talent," she advised, "and then settle down to work with it for a good long time." Find your aptitude and then "honor it" and "work with it."

> *Well, a little blunt, maybe, but it has the advantage of being direct. Let it stand and go on.*

So Shekerjian had a lead that honored her subject without scaring the reader away from it. And by including her internal debate, she gave us insight into how she created that lead.

If first is most important, what comes second?

You'll come to your lead from a variety of angles, using a variety of techniques and choosing from among an array of formats. But however you come to your lead, you'll know it's the most important bit of writing in the piece.

So it would seem to follow that the words immediately following the lead—the bridge into the body of the article or chapter—must be the second most important element. The bridge is important, all right. But we must reserve second place to the last words to appear in the piece, the conclusion.

Does that seem strange? Why would the last words the reader encounters be so important?

Two reasons. First, they may not be the last words she reads. Many readers, including graduates of the various speed-reading courses that have proliferated in a culture obsessed by time, learn to read first and last paragraphs, along with subtitles and topic sentences, in a quick initial scan, to grasp the main idea and decide whether to go back and read the whole piece. So the conclusion, along with the introduction, may determine whether the browser becomes a reader after all.

Suppose you were as intrigued by the opening passage of *Uncommon Genius* as I was, but not quite ready to commit to reading the whole book. You might flip to the back of the book, to see "how it turns out." If you did, you'd find this quote from MacArthur Fellow Ellen Stuart:

> "Here you are wantin' to know about cree-a-tivity. Lemme tell you somethin', baby. Carin' is where it's at. Trust me now because I know what I'm talkin' 'bout—you got a love for what you're doin' and everythin' else, all the rest of this cree-a-tivity stuff you're wonderin' 'bout, baby, it just comes."

Shekerjian had saved some of the best for last—not a dry summary but a scintillating quote, helping convince you to explore all the good stuff in the middle.

Here's another example of the bread—first and last statements—selling the sandwich. This title jumped out at me from the cover of a thin, unpretentious little volume: *How to Peel a Sour Grape: An Impractical Guide to Successful Failure*, by Richard P. Frisbie. Nice twist on the old sour grapes cliché, and an arresting oxymoron with "successful failure." A gimmick, or did this Frisbie fellow really have something to say? I opened to chapter one, "Failure knocks, and knocks, and knocks," and read:

Every man past a certain age, perhaps thirty-five, knows in his heart that he is a failure. He doesn't realize that almost everyone else is a failure, too.

Hardly standard self-help fare, which usually features a style perhaps best characterized as cheerleader-on-uppers. Intrigued, but not yet intrigued enough to plunk my money down, I turned to the last page, where I found this observation:

So there it is — you've failed in the world, failed at home, failed as a personality. You're a failure to the marrow of your bone. The ultimate test, then, is whether failure makes you bitter. The truth is that failure is a joke, not for the derision of demons, but the gentle laughter of the saints.

That was enough to convince me to invite Frisbie home with me and grant him my time and attention.

Five more reasons to save the second best for last

The conclusion is also the second most important element in the piece for the reader who actually begins at the beginning, plows straight through the middle, and comes out at the end, taking the piece in logical order. Here are five good reasons why:

• The lead makes the promise; the conclusion makes sure the reader knows that you kept the promise.
• The lead entices her to spend the time; the conclusion assures her it was time well spent (and prevents "buyer's remorse").
• The lead makes her want to read; the conclusion makes her glad she did.
• The lead convinces her to read this piece; the conclusion motivates her to read the next one you write.
• And finally, of everything she reads, she's most likely to remember the conclusion.

For all these reasons, and for others we'll discover together along the way, we'll need to focus as intently on endings as on beginnings.

As we do, we'll concentrate on making sure the lead and the conclusion share a unity of style and tone, that they create a satisfying frame for the article or chapter. We'll explore ways to let format and tone arise organically from subject and slant, from your sense of audience, and from your purpose in writing the piece.

We'll approach these two critical elements of any piece of nonfiction, the beginning and the ending, with respect for the reader's intelligence and gratitude for the precious gift of her time.

After all, she may have had no intention of stopping at our store.

Part One

GETTING YOUR LEAD TO CARRY ITS LOAD — WITHOUT BREAKING A SWEAT

CHAPTER ONE

Why You've Read a Lot More Leads Than Conclusions

Want to get humbled in a hurry? Make a list of all the things your reader could do instead of reading what you've worked so hard to write.

To start with, there are all the other things she really *should* read and reasons why she *should* read them, things like:

- a daily newspaper (to be an informed citizen),
- a weekly news magazine (to be an even more informed citizen),
- a community newspaper (to keep abreast of local issues/gossip),
- work-related publications (If she designs office space for a living, for example, she probably reads *Facilities Design & Management.* Writers are likely to read *Writer's Digest, Publisher's Auxiliary,* maybe the *New York Times Book Review,* the way a film mogul reads *Variety,* not simply for the pleasure and sense of community they bring, but to keep up on the trade.),
- tax preparation booklet (seasonal — ugh),
- office memos and annual reports (with us always, and double ugh) .

Now add in all the print that falls into the gray area between *should* and *want to,* things like:

- direct mail catalogs for products and services she's interested in,
- publications indirectly related to work (For a liquor distributor working the Wisconsin territory, for example, *On Premise,* the

Official Publication of the Tavern League of Wisconsin, would be a near-must.),
- parenting magazines,

let alone the things she'd really *like* to read, like:

- personal letters,
- novels, poetry, short stories, essays (fun stuff like *Wild Dog*, the magazine for "people determined to break loose from the paradigm," or *Out West*, "the newspaper that roams"),
- hobby and special interest publications (like *The Harmonizer*, for lovers of barbershop quartets, or *The Peoria Woman*, a marvelous regional magazine).

And that's just stuff to read. You're also competing with real life and all the activities your potential reader might want or need to do instead of reading anything at all, like playing badminton, walking the dog, watching television or making love.

You see what you're up against. Frightening, isn't it?

But this exercise in humility isn't designed to scare you into keyboard paralysis. It is designed to scare you just enough to help you focus on the vital question of how to create article and chapter leads so powerful and compelling, they draw the reader away from *Cigar Aficionado* and *Baseball America* (unless, of course, your article appears in *Cigar Aficionado* or *Baseball America*), away from badminton, away from the television, and into your words.

You can't draw all of the people all the time

To make the task a bit less daunting, we need to note four groups of readers you *aren't* creating your leads for:

1. *Folks who read your work because you wrote it,* including fans of previous work, close relatives, and very close friends. (You may not have as many of these as you thought you had before you published.)

2. *Folks who read your work because of the topic.* Put "baseball" in a headline or lead, and I'll start reading. I'll probably keep reading until and unless you ambush me with irrelevancies, dreadful writing or blatant inaccuracy, or until I realize that I've been tricked, that your piece is really about jai alai, for example, and not about baseball. I'm that big a fan.

3. *Folks who* won't *read your work because you wrote it.* You may have made a few "anti-fans" along the way, although I certainly hope not. More likely, some folks may avoid you because of what, not who, you are. I usually leave the "professor" off my byline, for example,

because I figure that some potential readers will smell moth-balled lecture notes, with essay exam to follow.

4. *Folks who won't read your work because of the topic.* I have a colleague and friend named Blake who is decidedly not a baseball fan. (He is otherwise a good and fine man. I'm at a loss to explain this major defect in his character.) If Blake spotted "baseball" in the headline or lead of the same article I so eagerly pursued, he'd surely pass it by.

Adorn it with social relevance:

Baseball as metaphor for modern society.

He'll still pass.

Float it in a sea of dollar signs:

Baseball's first $7 million second baseman.

Still no sale.

Stick an active verb in it:

Baseball bars the way for black managers.

It's still baseball, and it's still no go.

Render your baseball promise in four-color, three-dimension, scratch and sniff on coated paper that tastes like chocolate, has no calories, and supplies 100 percent of your daily requirement of riboflavin. Blake still won't bite.

You're not crafting your leads for any of the folks in these four categories. Those in the first two don't need the persuasion, and those in the latter two won't be swayed by it. You're writing for the seducibles, those who will give your writing a try if and only if you give them a good reason to. You're writing for the undecideds, the same folks who serve as the targets for all political advertising. Elections are decided by the "undecided" vote, and more and more of us list ourselves as "undecided" in each election.

Swear off "a meeting will be held"/ "a speech was given" leads forever

That means you just can't afford to lead with the trite and true. Every story, even the creaky old meeting advance story for the club newsletter, must have an inviting lead. Make that *especially* the meeting advance story. You may have written a lot of them; your reader may have read— or chosen not to read—a lot of them, too. Chances are she'll take a pass on this tired old format:

Convention to be held
The annual convention of the Association for the Preservation of the North American Coyote will be held on August 17-18 in Wendover, Nevada.

Ho hum. Nothing new here. Turn page.

To avoid this sort of non-lead lead, ask yourself what's different about a particular meeting. Then reflect the difference in your lead. Look at the way *Newsbeat*, the newsletter for the Southern Wisconsin Educational In-Service Organization, promoted its convention:

Convention to offer laughter, tears
Don't bring papers to grade while attending the SWEIO convention. Chances are they would become streaked with tears or otherwise marred during fits of uncontrollable laughter. . . . The two presenters signed so far promise an unforgettable day.

Avoid, too, the passive "a speech was given" lead. What did the speaker say? Put the essence in the lead, as Dianne Paley did in her lead for the *Wisconsin State Journal* coverage of a campaign speech in Madison.

"Do you vote?" demanded Barry Commoner, Citizen's Party candidate for president. "Of course you don't. How many times can you go into the polling booth holding your nose."

Whether you agree with or object to Commoner's view of democracy in America, you're likely to be engaged by it. Paley gives you the chance to react by leading with the essence.

She then covers the necessary information:
- where? — the Great Hall of the Memorial Union.
- when? — Sunday afternoon.
- why? — one of many stops on a national tour to drum up support for the Citizen's Party.

But before the browser wants the answers to these questions, she needs the answer to a more fundamental query: "So what?" She needs to know how the information relates to her. If you fail to address that question in the lead, you risk losing your potential reader.

Letting the reader participate

When I was assigned an article on the tax on long-distance telephone calls, a rather unappetizing prospect, I discovered that calling from Wisconsin to Minnesota cost more than making the same call from Minnesota to Wisconsin. Why? What can a Wisconsin resident do about it? The phone companies told me one thing, the Citizens' Utility Board another. I decided to pass the controversy — and, I hope, the energy — on to the reader in the lead:

> AT&T calls it a "Wisconsin tax adjustment."
> U.S. Sprint calls it a "sales/utility tax."
> MCI calls it a "state and local surcharge."
> What the Citizens' Utility Board (CUB) calls it you couldn't print in a magazine.
> No matter what you call it, if you operate a business in Wisconsin, you pay 12.23 percent more for every long-distance call you make out of state than do businesses in neighboring states.

I'm still quite fond of that lead and share it with you with no apologies. But as I now second-guess myself (where was all this wisdom when the page was blank?), I think I could have simply cut right to the essence, letting the "what's in it for the reader" leap out:

> If you operate a business in Wisconsin, you pay more for every long-distance call you make out of state than do your competitors in Minnesota, Iowa and Illinois.

When I wrote a profile of Lands' End, the direct mail pioneers based in Dodgeville, Wisconsin, I put together two bits of information to create a lead I hoped would involve the reader by letting her finish drawing the conclusion:

> Lands' End is celebrating its 25th anniversary this year.
> So is the ZIP code.
> This may not be a coincidence.

because Lands' End was one of the first companies to figure out how helpful the ZIP code — and the consumer demographics it generates — could be to a merchandiser.

How has this trend in marketing changed the nature of that pile of mail waiting for my reader at the end of a hard day?

> Before you dismiss it as junk mail, take a close look at that Lands' End catalog. . . . You don't just get it, you subscribe to it . . . . It looks like a magazine. It reads like a magazine. It promotes itself like a magazine. But it's a catalog, all right.

Picking the "right lead"

Preparing to write a profile on a fellow named Clark Wilkinson, who converted the basement of his Baraboo, Wisconsin, home into a Hollywood Film Museum, I assembled a hefty clip file. As I read through all the stories that had already been published on him, I was struck by the different approaches writers had taken to try to involve the reader.

For the general interest audience reading the *Milwaukee Journal*, this descriptive lead:

> "Welcome, monster lovers."
> With a gleaming white skull perched on it, this sign hangs over the door of the basement room of Clark Wilkinson's home here.

Another description, this one for a mass-market tourism publication, *Wisconsin Weekend* (with a little cheek-billowing alliteration thrown in for fun):

> In a bungalow basement in Baraboo the shades of King Kong and Frankenstein's daughter mingle with memories of Tom Mix, Greta Garbo and nearly every other Hollywoodian, present and past, since the movies began in 1889.

For the *St. Paul Pioneer Press*, a human interest focus:

> Clark Wilkinson, 66, a Baraboo insurance man, has a problem. He has, friends say, the most pronounced case of motion picture hobbyism in the annals of that delightful malady.

The *Milwaukee Sentinel*, perhaps worried that you've read it all before, tried to catch you leaning in the wrong direction:

> His skin is dry and cracked. His joints are creaky and he is beginning to lose his hair.
> At age 44, King Kong is showing his years.

The local *Baraboo News Republic* took the personal approach:

> The small sign directs me around to the back of the attractive brick ranch house where Clark Wilkinson and his wife, Muriel, sit in the cool afternoon air.

and again in another feature for a different issue:

> The mystique of Hollywood is just around the corner to residents of Baraboo. . . .

Veteran freelancer Al P. Nelson favored direct address:

> Would you like to live in a house with 10 glamorous movie queens, each clad in the expensive dress she wore in a historical movie spectacular? Of course, the movie queens are only lovely mannequins. . . .

A magazine of reminiscence, *Wisconsin Then and Now,* not surprisingly took the long view with this anecdotal lead:

> For Clark Wilkinson, it all started in 1915 as he sat in the Gem Theater in Baraboo and watched the story of "Rumplestiltskin" flicker across the screen.

Which lead is best? The best lead is appropriate for its subject, its publication and its audience. It convinces the skimmer to become a reader, induces the window shopper to come inside to browse. In short, *the right lead is the lead that works.* There is no one right lead. There are lots of possibilities. We'll explore those possibilities in the chapters to follow.

CHAPTER TWO

Creating the Power Lead

Saul Pett figured his job was really pretty simple. "Tell readers not only what happened," he would say, "but what it was like to have been there."

Pett wrote feature stories for the Associated Press from 1946 until his retirement in 1991. He profiled famous folk, including every sitting president from Harry Truman to George Bush, and a lot of plain folk, too. He won a Pulitzer in 1982 for his 8,500-word feature on the federal bureaucracy.

Eighty-five hundred words on the federal bureaucracy? And people read it? And gave him a prize for it?

That's how good Saul Pett was.

He managed in the first seventy-six words to capture the essence of that lumbering mastodon we call "Uncle Sam":

> The government of the United States is so big you can't say where it begins and where it ends. It is so shapeless you can't diagram it with boxes because, after you put the president here and the Congress there and the judiciary in a third place, where in the hell do you put the Ad Hoc Committee for the Implementation of PL89-306? Or the Interdepartmental Screw Thread Committee? Or the Interglacial Panel on the President?

That, friends, is a power lead. It delivers subject, slant and attitude. (He's kidding about the Interdepartmental Screw Thread Committee. Isn't he?)

Pett addresses us directly, in a friendly, conversational tone, and uses common words. None of that "one can't extrapolate a true commencement or termination" stuff for Pett. The only tough words are "implementation," "interdepartmental" and maybe "interglacial," and we don't really need to know what they mean to get the point. Besides, they're in there precisely because they're a mouthful, and thus indicative of the bloat and bloviation inherent in the government.

Pett draws us a picture. Imagine an endless organizational chart, with little committee boxes sliding off the page, tumbling over the rim of the table and into your lap.

All this in seventy-six words.

One paragraph later, Pett defies Mark Twain's great dictum, "If you can catch an adjective, kill it," shattering just about every piece of good advice ever given about proper sentence length as he personifies the bureaucracy as,

> A big, bumbling, generous, naive, inquisitive, acquisitive, intrusive, meddlesome giant with a heart of gold and holes in his pockets, an incredible hulk, a 10-ton marshmallow lumbering along an uncertain road of good intentions somewhere between capitalism and socialism, an implausible giant who fights wars, sends men to the moon, explores the ends of the universe, feeds the hungry, heals the sick, helps the helpless, a thumping complex of guilt trying mightily to make up for past sins to the satisfaction of nobody. . . a malleable, vulnerable colossus pulled every which way by everybody who wants a piece of him, which is everybody.

Reading that monster nonsentence is like trying to ride a 40-foot wave. The sheer force carries you along, but if you slip off the curl, you'll surely drown under tons of churning water. Pett violates all sense of propriety intentionally, of course, letting his prose rage just barely this side of out-of-control because his subject rages just barely this side of out-of-control. Form matches content. We don't just get it with our heads, we feel it in our guts.

That's a power lead.

But that's not the only way Pett knew to write. To profile the writer Dorothy Parker, Pett adopted a style more like Hemingway than Faulkner. The bureaucracy merited a tidal wave; Parker got this round of machine-gun fire:

> "Are you married, my dear?"
> "Yes, I am."
> "Then you won't mind zipping me up."
> Zipped up, Dorothy Parker turned to face her interviewer and

the world. She wore a polka dot dress and pearls and, characteristically, her black gray hair in bangs, her mouth in a small girl smile, her big, round, brown eyes in a look of startled innocence.

Zipped up and now sipping her Scotch neat, she confirmed an ugly rumor that seems to surprise both young and old: Dorothy Parker has turned 70.

Another power lead, nothing like the first example. Form serves content. We experience Dorothy Parker.

Pett the reporter was nowhere to be seen in the first piece. In the second, he interacted with his subject, however briefly ("Yes, I am."), because he needed to be there to make it work.

In the first lead, Pett pulled out trick after word trick of sound and image. In the second, he used only one subdued scrap of irony (Dorothy Parker was anything but "zipped up" mentally).

Pett did whatever he needed to do to make the lead work, to convey the essence and render the reader unable or at least unwilling to resist reading on. That's the power in a power lead, the force that convinces the browser, of her own free will, to set down her life, still the murmurings of preoccupation, and become a reader.

A fellow tries out for a part in his church's production of *West Side Story* and winds up landing the role of Riff, the leader of the Jets, one of the rival gangs in the remake of *Romeo and Juliet*. Who cares, right? But this particular amateur actor happens to be Rob Hoerburger, editor of *The New York Times Magazine*. He knows his way around a lead, knows to look for the element of surprise:

> I walked into the confessional a repentant sinner and walked out a dancer.

Huh?

> The priest who heard my sins half-jokingly suggested that for my penance I join the church's production of "West Side Story," which he was directing.

Ah.

On the particular July Sunday morning when I encountered this lead, I was steaming happily through the magazine, working my way rapidly back to my Sunday treat, the crossword puzzle. (Oh, what a rare and glorious day, when I actually solve *The New York Times Magazine* crossword!) I didn't want to stop and read an article on *West Side Story*. I resented the obstacle between me and my puzzle. I read the article anyway.

That's a power lead.

Hal Holbrook is coming to town to re-create his classic one-man show, *Mark Twain Tonight*. A good show, yes, but he's been doing it for forty years, after all. What could you possibly say in an advance story that hasn't been said before?

Maybe the very fact that he's been doing it for forty years.

> Hal Holbrook has been playing Mark Twain on stage for 40 years.

Well, yes. I suppose that's admirable and all. But there's no power to it. Lots of folks have been standing the same watch for that long, and nobody writes articles about them for the newspaper, let alone pays good money to see them perform.

But put a slight twist on the same information, as Michael Kilian did for this lead for the *Chicago Tribune*, and you've got a power lead:

> Hal Holbrook has been Mark Twain for nearly as long as Samuel Clemens was.

Those few words resonate with irony and insight, reminding us that Clemens, no less than Holbrook, was playing a role.

For his review of the Scott Turow novel *Pleading Guilty* for *The New York Times Book Review*, John Mortimer delivered a surprising burst of insight in this power lead:

> The great detectives have one thing in common. They almost never have sex.

I'd never thought of that.

A piece on "the battle against baldness" for *Business Week* draws us in with star power and then explodes:

> People can say it's a sign of virility, talk all they want about such sex symbols as Telly Savalas and Sean Connery. But for the average man, going bald is an experience he'd rather have happen to the next guy.

And it probably will.

Seven elements of a power lead

Just what, then, is a power lead, that marvelous storefront display that converts a window shopper into a customer?

1. *The power lead offers the reader something she wants.* "Come on in," the lead coos or bubbles or challenges, "and I will inform you, inspire you, entertain you, maybe make you laugh right out loud."

The lead does *not* promise to change the reader's mind, to teach her a valuable lesson, or otherwise "improve her" or tell her something she really *needs* to know (in the opinion of the writer). That's more threat than promise. Most of us like our minds pretty much the way they are.

2. *The power lead is appropriate to the material.* Style, tone and diction all serve the cause. Without sacrificing clarity, the lead sets the proper mood. A bloated bureaucracy gets a bloated lead. Snippy Dorothy Parker gets staccato bursts.

3. *The power lead is unforced.* It emerges organically from the material, rather than being imposed from outside. No irrelevant jokes followed by a lame "but seriously, folks" bridge. No prefabricated houses, no precooked dinners, no boilerplate specials, and no fair using the great metaphor you couldn't find a place for in your last piece.

4. *The power lead is original.* If the lead truly emerges from the specific material, and if it is truly appropriate to that material, it can be like no other lead, because no other lead ever had to fit this particular set of circumstances.

5. *The power lead is concise.* Take another look at Saul Pett's long lead on the bureaucracy. A lot of words, yes? But could you cut any of them without taking away from the mood, the rhythm and the sense? A power lead may be two words or two hundred or more, but however many words there are, every word needs to be there.

6. *The power lead is specific and concrete.* "Federal bureaucracy" is an abstraction. A 10-ton marshmallow is tangible. We can't see or taste or touch or smell a bureaucracy. We can wallow in a giant marshmallow until we suffocate.

7. *The power lead works.* It may not fit any of these other criteria. It may break all the rules. It may defy explanation or analysis. But it works. It inspires the browser to read more.

And three things a power lead *isn't*

1. *A power lead isn't "creative"* if by "creative" we mean self-conscious or contrived.

2. *A power lead isn't cute or clever* if by clever we mean that the lead calls attention to its own technique.

3. *A power lead isn't obtrusive* in the same way that just enough of a subtle perfume does the job without ever calling attention to itself.

We don't want the reader thinking "What a terrific lead!" (We certainly don't want her thinking "What a rotten lead!" either.) We don't want her thinking about the lead at all. We want her to forget she's reading and abandon herself to the ideas and images we've assembled for her.

If you want to learn what a power lead is and isn't, start paying close attention to the leads you encounter in your own reading. Read consistently excellent and innovative publications (like the wonderful magazine and book review sections that come with each week's Sunday *New York Times*). Clip the leads that work particularly well for you and figure out how they did it.

Study rotten leads, too, explaining their failures to your own satisfaction. Rewrite the ones that didn't quite work. Second-guessing is a traditional and honorable way to become a better writer.

I've assembled a lot of good and bad leads for you, and in the chapters that follow, we'll look at both the triumphs and the tragedies.

CHAPTER THREE

Taking the Pressure Off

I spent many precious hours while in college playing pool.

I know. All those hours would have been better spent at the library. But at the time, it seemed very important that I master topspin and backspin, the bank shot and the break shot, the delicate art of leaving myself with good shape on the next shot or my opponent with no shape at all.

Anybody who thought I lacked self-discipline in those days should have seen me laboring with a pool cue in my hands.

I managed to become proficient at nine-ball, winning about as often as I lost. But I could never beat John Spitzer, not on my best day or his worst.

We called him The Iowa Kid, because he came from Iowa City, and because the name seemed appropriate for a pool hustler, which Johnny surely was. He shot a fine stick, as they say. But so did some of the other young men who gathered in the smoky poolroom just off the dining room of my frat house. What set The Iowa Kid apart, I have come to understand, was the mental game.

John never seemed to rattle. If he worried about a shot, it never showed. The tighter the match, the higher the stakes, the cooler Johnny got.

When it came your turn to shoot against him, he might stand just at the edge of vision, cigarette dangling from his lips, and as you bent to line up your shot, he might murmur, "Don't miss. Remember who's shooting next."

You might miss, he was clearly implying, but *he* wouldn't. He was reminding you that he was waiting to shoot next, yes, but more importantly, he recalled you to the reality that *you* were shooting *now*. Instead of concentrating on the shot, you were now concentrating on your own terrible need to make that shot, an entirely different thing.

Nothing, of course, could be more detrimental to a clear eye and a steady hand.

Imagine yourself no longer in the smoky poolroom but instead out on the mound in the center of a baseball diamond. You stand alone, facing the opposition's most dangerous batter. The bases are loaded, the game on the line. A mistake now means a certain loss. You grip the ball, peering in for the sign from your catcher. The fans are screaming, an inarticulate wave of noise threatening to wash you away. The batter glares out at you and swings the bat menacingly. You take a deep breath, noticing as you do that the third baseman is trotting over to give you a quick word of encouragement and a chance to catch a few more seconds of rest.

He reaches the mound, takes the ball from you, and rubs it up while looking out toward left field. He turns, grins, flips the ball to you, and says, "Don't blow it, you idiot! Your whole career is riding on this pitch."

No, no, no. He's supposed to say something about it just being a little game of pitch and catch, about there being no batter up there, about you having seven good teammates out there behind you. Or maybe he should talk about plans to go out after the game, something, anything, to take your mind off the dread confrontation still waiting for you at the plate.

"Go with the force," Obi Wan tells Luke Skywalker in the first *Star Wars* film. Don't think about hitting the target. Don't think at all. Just feel. Trust to instinct.

Ten tips your Zen Master never taught you about writing leads

So, we're agreed. Leads are extremely important.

Now, sit down and try to write one.

In the first two chapters, I've handed you the ball and, in essence, said, "Don't blow it. The first twenty-five words are the most important you'll ever write. Your whole career as a writer depends on them."

Now you're going to relax, forget all about the importance of it all, and let the words flow.

Obi Wan slays writer's block.

The first few words the reader encounters are important, yes. But the first few words you write aren't necessarily important at all, because the reader will probably never see them.

Getting started is tough. Wrestling yourself down in front of the typewriter or computer and risking all by putting words to paper can be terrifying, even for veteran writers, even for folks who love to write. But that's because we're looking for the "right place to start," the magic words that will free us from our anxieties and pull us into the writing just as surely as we hope they'll pull a reader in when we're finished.

So we create "writer's block," a wall of resistance to doing the work and paying the price, or "writer's blank," a vague emptiness from not knowing what to write or how to write it.

But there isn't a right place to start. *It doesn't matter where you start. It only matters* that *you start.* Start anywhere. Write anything. You'll write your way to where you need to be.

Deadline writers know this. If they don't write, they don't eat. So they write. The words come. Sometimes they stream out happily like kids tumbling out of the car in the parking lot at Disneyland, and the writer feels elated. Sometimes the words must be pulled out painfully, like reluctant children forced to keep an appointment with the dentist. The writing takes forever on those bad days, and the writer is sure the writing stinks.

But either way, the writing gets done. Either way, it will need revising.

There are no secrets, beyond the revelation that a good start is any start at all. But there are techniques, ways to help you get over the jitters and get started. None of these ten techniques need take more than a few moments, but they may save hours—and a lot of stress.

1. *Collect beginnings before you begin.* Practice this technique consistently and you may never need the other nine.

Look for leads as you gather your material, conduct your interviews, plan your approach. Keep constantly open to possibilities. You may consciously uncover a good lead or, more likely, several of them. Or your subconscious, playing with the possibilities while you sleep or jog or shower or work a crossword puzzle or listen to classical music, may thrust an idea into consciousness with an excited "Look at this! Isn't this terrific!"

Jot down such gifts as they occur. But don't type them up and send them off to the editor. You're still dealing with possibilities, not final copy.

2. *Play "How many ways?"* Instead of looking for the one right way to begin, thus pressuring your creativity into a coma, create several

possible ways. You can come back and select the most useful one when you're done.

Set a quota of five or ten or a dozen first sentences or paragraphs. Write as fast as you can. Don't stop short of your goal, and don't evaluate your attempts as you create them.

Some writers fill their quotas by going over their notes, auditioning good quotes, meaningful anecdotes, startling statements and surprising statistics for the lead role. Others put their notes aside and create from memory, trusting that they'll remember important themes and images.

You may find yourself coming back to your first idea. Well and good. The time you spent developing the other eleven won't be wasted. (Creative time is *never* wasted. How better to be living?) You'll have affirmed your original instinct and explored other notions that may serve you later in the piece. But you may also find your lead in the ninth or eleventh or eighteenth idea on your list. You never would have discovered it if you'd settled for the first "right" answer. That's why some writers play the "How many ways?" game even when they don't feel stuck.

3. *Play "Beat the clock."* Same game, slightly different rules. Instead of a quota, set a time limit. See how many notions you can generate in a ten- or fifteen-minute sprint.

Play this game if it frees you from self-conscious worry and helps you lose yourself in ideas and images. But if you constantly hear the ticking of the clock—just another sneaky way to force you to think about yourself, after all—"Beat the clock" isn't for you.

4. *Sit right down and write yourself a letter.* Banish the editor and the critic. Don't let the English teacher look at your draft. Write for a friend, or for yourself. Talk about what you want to talk about. Try out a word, a phrase, an idea. A good friend will forgive you your digressions. A very good friend will even enjoy a walk with you for the sake of the company, with no apparent destination. (Can you be that sort of very good friend for yourself as you write?)

You may emerge from your few minutes of meandering with a marvelous lead. You may not, but you'll have clarified your thinking, refocused your energy, and readied yourself to try one of the other techniques on our list.

5. *Create a "tornado outline."* If the thought of writing an outline makes your guts tighten and your resolve loosen, you're not alone. I never fared very well with all those Roman numerals and items in parallel structure, either.

But a "tornado outline" (also called "bubble" or "tree" or "spoke" outline and a lot of other names) isn't about parallel structure. It's a free and easy way to take mental inventory. Ideas on the page become tangible, and you can begin to discover connections. Structure emerges from seeming chaos.

Get away from the word processor or typewriter. (That in itself can be liberating if you spend a lot of time at a keyboard.) Get a sheet of paper, preferably a big one, maybe even a piece of what we used to call butcher paper (before meat began magically appearing packaged with clear plastic wrap). Put your subject in the middle of the sheet (immediately abolishing the tyranny of the upper-left corner). Jot down ideas as they occur to you, in no particular order (because it's order you're trying to discover). When you think you've pretty well exhausted the supply, sit still, pen or pencil or crayon in hand, and wait to see if more ideas want to come. When you're fairly sure you've drained the well, begin looking for themes, for associations, for related images. Draw lines and circles connecting them.

Your "outline" will look like as if a tornado hit an alphabet factory (thus the name, I suppose). But it will enable you to discover what you know and what you need to know, and it may point you to your lead.

6. *Play "Twenty questions."* You may have gotten stuck in your point of view. (What does this material mean to me?) If so, a quick game of twenty questions will get you unstuck. What does the material mean to your reader? How is it relevant to her life? What would she most like to know? Create a list of reader questions. Write them all down, no matter how seemingly farfetched. Try to remember your own ignorance before you began researching your subject. What misconceptions did you have (which is to say, what did you know for sure that you now know for sure just isn't true)? If your reader could interview the folks you've talked to, what would she ask?

Look through your list of questions. Do themes emerge? Does one question or group of related questions emerge as clearly more important than the others? Will the answer to one question serve as a proper foundation for further exploration? As you explore these questions, you discover your lead.

7. *Make a picture.* Folks who scoop ice cream all day get sick of ice cream. Projectionists stop watching the movie. And writers get word bound.

You may need to get away from words for a while. Silence the yammering word-maker inside you. Listen to music. Take a walk. Shoot baskets out on the driveway (humorist Dave Barry's diversion of choice). Come back to the keyboard or tablet, sit quietly for a few minutes, and make mental pictures of your subjects.

You might begin with a still life and move gently into a movie. You might start with a fuzzy outline and add detail and clarity. You may start out making the pictures but soon find yourself experiencing them instead. Let this happen. It is a very good thing indeed.

When you feel ready to write, seek words for the pictures you've experienced.

8. *Warm up.* Imagine yourself back out on that pitcher's mound, the game on the line, the opposing team's slugger waiting at the plate. (We'll leave that idiot third baseman out of it this time.) But this time suppose you've just come into the game, in relief of the starting pitcher, and you haven't had time to throw a single warm-up pitch. You not only have to throw the pitch of your life, you have to throw it without getting arm, legs and head ready.

No manager would be crazy enough to put you into a situation like that. But you may be doing it to yourself when you sit down to write.

Just as an athlete warms up before competing, some writers need to limber up with a few minutes of writing aerobics. Writing is a physical as well as a mental activity. You might just need to get your fingers moving. Type the lead story from this morning's sports page or a paragraph or two from a favorite book. Retype the last page of your own stuff from your last writing session.

"Free-write," pouring out whatever's on your mind. Free-writing not only warms up fingers and mind but clears out potential distractions. Instead of trying to ignore the buzzings of your mind, give them expression and thus expel them.

Take a slip from your "funny first lines" jar, copy it, and write two more paragraphs, seeing where the words take you. What's that? You don't have a "funny first lines" jar? Start collecting first lines, then, from the media and from your imagination. I've gotten them from television shows like *WKRP in Cincinnati* ("The Senator was at a loss to explain his nudity"); from a street preacher who liked to harangue university students on a mall near my office ("The Reverend Jed liked to tell the story of how he found Christ in a Burger King"); from my own brainstorming (as when an exercise to find a title for my first writing book for Writer's Digest Books, *Freeing Your Creativity,* led me to discover the title for my second book, *How to Write with the Skill of a Master and the Genius of a Child*).

9. *Start anywhere but at the beginning.* Directors almost always shoot the scenes of a movie out of sequence. All location scenes are shot at one time, to save on the time and expense of travel. All the scenes with the protagonist sporting a beard are shot before he shaves. The director may not always be entirely sure what order the scenes will ultimately assume.

In the same way, you don't have to begin at the beginning and write straight through to the end. If you aren't ready to write the lead, begin wherever you're comfortable. If you know where you want to wind up but aren't sure how you'll get there, write the end first.

Often you'll write yourself into your lead early on in the process. Your lead may be the last bit you write. You may find yourself with a disjointed mound of unconnected sections, but this mound is considerably better than nothing. Assemble your pieces, smooth over the seams, and polish your prose. The reader will never know, or care, what order you wrote the material in, as long as the prose moves smoothly and logically.

10. *Write left-handed, with blunt crayon, on tree bark.* Most writers I know of keep regular writing hours and compose in the same place, in the same way, every day. That way, the familiarity and routine sustain them through the hard times.

For some it's an early morning date with the word processor in a corner of the basement. For others, it's a notepad, a #2 pencil and the seashore. Some must have silence, while others crave background noise. Some are sprinters, working for no more than fifteen or twenty minutes at a stretch. Others immerse themselves in intense writing marathons. Whatever the pattern, the discipline and regularity help them write freely and productively.

But routine can become rut. Occasionally you may need to turn your schedule on its ear. Write at a different time, in a different place, with a different implement. Then, when you find yourself becoming impatient, when you long again for that boring old computer on that boring old desk, you're ready to reembrace your routine and lose yourself in the writing.

However you approach the task, and no matter how you feel about it when you sit down to write, develop a sense of purposeful play. Take chances. Write from all of yourself. Hold nothing back for next time. There will always be more where that came from. Give yourself permission to fail, because there can truly be no failure, only the work itself, with joy as much in the doing as in the having done.

CHAPTER FOUR

Getting Out of the Way

"Nobody cares what storms you've encountered but only that you brought the ship safely into port."

I gleaned that bit of cynical wisdom from a sign in the window of a liquor store near my office. With a bit of paraphrasing, it might describe the reader's attitude toward your writing:

"I don't care how long or hard you worked. I don't care that you had a cold while you wrote or that you had to pass up the movie you'd been looking forward to all week to meet your deadline. I don't care how you felt about the writing while you were writing it. I don't care how much you got paid, how many publishing credits you've got, what awards you have or have not won. I only care that the writing interests, informs or entertains me."

"This month I would like to do something just a little different," a columnist for a fine Illinois city magazine begins, "and about as near and dear to me as hearth and home."

But why should the reader care that your approach is "near and dear" to you? "Come to the point," the reader demands—if you're lucky. If you're not so lucky, she simply skips on to something else.

The writing isn't about the writer. Your reader shouldn't be thinking about you, not even to think how clever you are (although in your heart of hearts, you probably wish she would).

"I cannot stand journalists who write in the first person," Kenneth Arbogast wrote (in the first person) for the "Shop Talk" column in *Editor & Publisher* magazine. He cited the hard-bitten editor who threw a piece of self-absorbed copy back at the writer with the admonition, "Here, here. You left out what you ate for lunch."

When we insert ourselves unnecessarily into the writing, we create what Arbogast called "Hey, look at me" writing. Mary Benedict, professor emeritus of journalism from Indiana University, dubbed it "I-sore" writing. Kevin Cook, writing for *Playboy*, discussed a current trend toward what he called "ego journalism," where the writer outshines the celebrity in the celebrity profile.

Lawyer turned sportscaster Howard Cosell invariably introduced a quote with a "When I had dinner with the champ last night, the champ said to me. . . . " preface, a clear example of ego journalism. Political commentator Rush Limbaugh does the same sort of thing, invariably interrupting his callers to soar into his own flights of oratory, "with half my brain tied behind my back," as he's so fond of announcing, "just to make it fair."

What's wrong with that? Why shouldn't the writer share (or even hog) the spotlight? Cosell and Limbaugh became celebrities, made pots of money, and put books on the bestseller list. (And the guy telling you to stay out of the spotlight has done none of those things.)

Maybe it works for Cosell and Limbaugh, but it might not work for you, and I'm certain it wouldn't work for me. Did you begin to read this book to learn more about me? You might have checked my credentials, to help you decide whether I was likely to know what I'm talking about, but I'll bet you decided to read this book because you wanted to learn about writing leads and conclusions, not about the "Life and Times of Marshall Cook."

As entertaining as Cosell might have been, I was always a lot more interested in what Muhammad Ali had to say than how Cosell got him to say it. And as fine a writer as Thomas Hauser assuredly is, I read his biography of Ali to find out about Ali, not about Hauser. (Hauser didn't disappoint me.)

But surely we have much to learn from autobiographies and from largely autobiographical essays, such as the quite personal and quite fine books on writing by Natalie Goldberg, Brenda Ueland, George Higgins, Ray Bradbury and so many others. We do, indeed. And if you can tell the story of your life in such a way that it has meaning and application for me, I'll gladly read it, and consider the time well spent. But take care not to weave the story of your life into your writing unless that story has a legitimate place there.

A student humor magazine called *The Onion*, which circulates on the campus where I work, recently published a parody review of the movie *Huck Finn*, by one "Archie 'Arch' Danielson. The piece describes Danielson's efforts to get to the Bijou, buy gumdrops and a soda ("so expensive it cost more than the movie did!"), find his seat, and deal with his rampaging nephew, Troy. ("I told him to pipe down and stop his bawling, but he wouldn't.")

"I didn't even get to see much of The Huck Finn Movie," the reviewer admits, "but from what I saw, it didn't look too good anyway."

The movie review gets lost in the reviewer's self-absorption.

The Onion was kidding, but this reporter for a suburban daily newspaper wasn't. He avoids the "I" word but lapses into "Look at me" writing even without it. The article's headline promises a profile of a teacher who "works for the community's youth" and "spreads special kind of cheer." But the lead delivers a slice of the writer's life:

> The interview with Reston teacher [name omitted] was scheduled to begin punctually at 11 a.m.
>
> Her visitor—whose familiarity with [her] career was somewhat limited—searched vainly for just the right, trenchant questions.

Honestly, do you care when the interview was scheduled to begin? Do you even have to know that an interview took place? (For that matter, do you know what "trenchant" means? Just thought I'd ask.) The writer not only inserts himself into the lead, blocking our view of the subject for two precious paragraphs, he also admits his lack of preparation ("familiarity" is "limited," the interviewer has no idea how he will begin the interview).

It's as if an after-dinner speaker began with, "I really don't know a whole lot about this subject, but . . ."

Pardon me while I head for the exit.

You have to take down the scaffold after you paint the house

Here's another way we sometimes block our reader's view of the subject. Suppose you own a beautiful old two-story Victorian house that is badly in need of painting, and you decide to dedicate a summer to the job. You pick your colors, erect your scaffold, spend sweaty days scraping and priming, and apply two coats of the finest exterior semi-gloss money can buy.

You finish just as the leaves are beginning to turn and the night air is developing a bit of a bite. You wash out your brushes, stow your paint and drop cloths, clean up the chips of old paint that have collected at the base of the house.

And you walk away, leaving the scaffold up. Folks drive by, glance at your house, and remark, "Look at that scaffold. Wonder what it's doing there?" or "Guess that guy's still painting his house. You'd think he'd be done by now."

They never see the house.

Your interview questions, your preliminary research, and your thought process are the scaffold. If you leave them in the writing, you block the reader's view of the subject.

Don't forget to take down the scaffold after you paint the house.

Let the reader see the painting for herself

Suppose you've purchased a beautiful painting (or, if you're in my league, a print of a beautiful painting). You cloak your treasure and invite friends over for the grand unveiling. You stand before the crowd and describe the painting at great length — the nuances of color and shading, the exquisite composition, the attention to detail. You speak intensely of the emotion the painting inspires in you.

And all the while, your friends are wondering when you're going to step aside, draw the curtain, and let *them* see the painting.

Here's a writer for a Wisconsin weekly newspaper "standing in the way of the painting" in his lead for a story on his first hang-gliding adventure:

> Well, I finally did it. I finally got up the courage to attempt unpowered flight. To dare to go where people have gone before. To take to the air on a wing and a prayer. Floating on the capricious breezes, the earth my enemy, the sky my quest.

We don't actually get to the hang-gliding class until the fourth paragraph, and we don't become airborne until midway through the article. And after all that, the writer tells us, "I'd like to be able to describe what an incredible feeling it is as you find yourself being lifted off the ground." But he can't, or won't, or at least doesn't. Instead of re-creating the experience, he simply tells us, at great length, how he felt about doing it, every step of the way. *He talks about the painting, but he never shows the painting to us.*

We still can't improve on Joseph Conrad's classic advice. You must let the reader *see*. Don't write about the painting or experience or conversation or idea. Write the painting, the experience, the conversation, the idea.

But what if the writer is the star?

Is there never a time, then, for the writer to appear in the writing? Sure there is. Consider the opening of this travel piece by Donald Baer, which appeared in the *U.S. News 1993 Great Vacation Drives*:

> Florida has always been many things to me, none of them particularly appealing. Too crowded; too old; too clichéd. . . . The

place seems better suited to the pages of a glossy magazine than the itinerary of an actual getaway. . . . I have always suspected this land of spring training and retirement villages would be just plain boring for a long drive.

Here's writer as adventurer, getting his bias out in the open right up front before taking you along on a journey that will (obviously) change his mind, and perhaps yours, about Florida. Baer could have tried to hide — "One may think of Florida as many things, none of them particularly appealing." But that would only weaken the writing.

Lewis Lord's offering in the same volume reinforces the point:

> Basic cravings pull visitors like me to Nashville, and there I was, resisting them all. I shunned Twitty City, avoided Tootsie's Orchid Lounge and ignored Ernest Tubb's Record Shop. I even skipped a chance to tour Barbara Mandrell Country and gawk at the nightie she wore to her wedding bed. Sure, I wanted to stay and stare, but the start of 450 miles of unspoiled Southern scenery and turbulent American history beckoned on the outskirts of town.

Opinion pieces of all sorts rely on a strong presence. It's pretty tough and often phony to try to write an experience piece without writing about yourself: "One could feel the bracing snap of the sea breeze as one leaned far out over the railing. . . ." Who's this "one" person doing all this sailing?

A few pages back, I told you I wanted to read about Muhammad Ali, not about his biographer. But when Davis Miller profiled Ali, he focused on his relationship with the Champ. Here the author's presence is necessary, and Miller appears almost immediately:

> In a suite on the 24th floor of the Mirage Hotel, Muhammad Ali is sitting on a small white sofa near full-length windows that overlook much of the east side of Las Vegas. He's wearing a pair of well-pressed, dark pinstripe slacks and a white, V-necked T-shirt that has a couple of nickel-size holes in it, one of which reveals whorls of thin white hair on the left side of his chest. His waist is very thick; I'd guess he weighs about 265.
>
> "My man," he said. "Glad to see you."
>
> Ali and I go back a long way.

But even in a first-person narration such as Miller's, the spotlight is clearly on Ali. Miller puts us in the hotel room and lets us see and hear the man for ourselves.

No predigested dinners

Writer-as-hero can get in the way of the writing. So can writer-as-mother-bird.

When a mother bird feeds her babies, she first — and there's just no delicate way to say this — digests the food herself and then — oh, dear, this really is rather gross — regurgitates it. It all makes sense if you're a baby bird, because you just aren't ready to digest for yourself. Mama must do it for you.

Our readers may not know what we're talking about until we tell them — that's what a great deal of nonfiction writing is all about, after all — but they aren't baby birds. They're quite capable of digesting for themselves.

We probably don't need to explain, put in context, draw the big picture, or in any other way predigest-and-regurgitate as often as we think we do. *And over-explanation can get in the way.* Take this lead for an article on day care in the workplace from another of Wisconsin's weekly newspapers:

> Before the 1970s, the world of work was, for the most part, considered a man's domain. However, in the past decade and a half, women have made a competent niche for themselves in the labor force.

We probably already knew that and thus don't really profit from the quick history lesson. This isn't really what the article is about anyway. The true subject comes in the next sentence, thirty-six precious words into the piece:

> And now, in what seems to be a natural progression, kids are coming along on the job.

That lead is like the after-dinner speaker who begins with this sort of throat clearing: "I want to thank you all for coming tonight. It's a real pleasure to see so many of you, here to explore a topic of utmost importance to us all and to the future of this great country of ours." Nervous speakers do this sort of thing all the time, calming their butterflies with the sound of their own voices uttering meaningless phrases.

Writers do it, too. I often clear my throat on the keyboard when I begin writing. It's a way to warm up and tell myself what I want to talk about and what I want to say about it. It's a form of writer aerobics. Eventually I start talking to the reader instead of to myself. But I have to remind myself to go back and hit the delete to get rid of all those preliminary mutterings.

That article on day care would have gotten off to a much more powerful start by cutting all the way down to "Kids are coming along on the job" for its lead.

The metaphor that devoured Cleveland

Another sort of ego journalism involves allowing language to become a barrier to understanding rather than a tool for achieving communion between reader and idea. Here's an example, from the fashion pages of *The New York Times*, dateline Paris:

> Karl Lagerfeld hit a home run today in his third time at bat here and won the ball game for Chanel.

A company softball game, perhaps, with the Chanels battling the Stetsons? Nope. It's a discussion of "wild, wicked" winter fashion designs, complete with the cheery news that "legs are back." You'll search in vain through the black tights and boots, the black velvet jackets "cut short to let the shirttail show," or even the jeans and jackets decorated with red braid stitching, to find anybody trying to leg a double into a triple. The metaphor doesn't grow from the material. It's imposed by a writer straining for a clever lead. So it gets in the way.

It can also get out of control, as when this sports writer for a Michigan daily gets all tangled up in clichés:

> The star-crossed Marinette Legion baseball team was on a collision course with Murphy's Law at the 66th annual Wisconsin American State Baseball Tournament.
>
> The Post 39 squad sailed into the fifth inning Monday night with a 1-0 lead against Janesville before the wheels came off on its ill-fated tournament drive.

Trusting self and reader

In the lead of her review of a science book for *The New York Times Book Review*, writer/teacher Ann Finkbeiner offers one explanation for the sort of forced cleverness that infects much of the writing she deals with:

> The current style in writing popular science is all breathlessness and black net stockings. No verb goes unadverbed. Chapters begin and end with one-sentence stunners. . . . Scientists have litter-strewn offices, impish fits of whimsy and big, dizzying views of infinity; they pore excitedly over data and peer avidly into the heavens.

Why all the language fireworks?

> The style would be over-sequined but innocuous except for its

implicit assumption: science is so arcane, so boring that no one will go inside unless there's cooch girls out front.

It's a matter, then, of trust. You *must* trust the subject to be worthy of time and effort—yours and the reader's. You must trust yourself to write clearly and honestly. And you must trust the reader to participate in the vision. If any of these three trust elements is lacking, you should probably go on to another project. In any event, you should never try to cover the hole with fancy wallpaper.

Lead, follow, or get out of the way

Sometimes the story needs your help to get itself told. We spend a great deal of time, after all, exploring techniques for developing a good lead, one that allows the story to unfold naturally. That search can take a lot of effort.

But often the best thing we can do for a story is simply to step aside and let it begin. Such is the case for Gina Kolata's brilliant lead on a health/ecology story for *The New York Times*:

> A new cancer drug that can melt away tumors that resist all other treatments has been found to help many more patients than researchers had realized. But very few people will get the drug because its only source is the bark of a sparsely distributed tree in the Pacific Northwest.

Here's the prototype story of our age—the search for a cancer cure smacks full speed into the need to protect the environment, in this case the rare, one hundred-year-old Pacific yew tree. Kolata doesn't bring in baseball metaphors, and she doesn't insert her own concerns or attitudes into the story. She simply lays out the dilemma in a two-sentence, fifty-word lead.

And how could you possibly improve on this incredible lead, underplayed by an Associated Press writer?

> A registered nurse pregnant with her first child jumped to her death from a tower in an abandoned train yard, but the infant survived after being delivered by two firefighters at the scene.

The writer had the grace to get out of the way and let the reader experience the drama.

Handling a story with this sort of restraint takes no less "creativity" than does the search for an effective metaphor or vital description. Creativity means solving a problem. The problem in any lead is how best to communicate with and involve the reader in the story.

I have no idea how hard the writer may have had to work to come up with this lead. It may have been the first lines to appear on the computer screen. It may have developed after long thought, an outline, and dozens of trips to the delete button. All I as a reader know and need to know is that the nurse died, the baby lived, and I should read on for the details.

Here's another AP paradigm of restraint, datelined Vinton, Louisiana:

> The preacher who crashed a carload of naked Pentecostals into a tree pleaded guilty to misdemeanor traffic charges Wednesday and was allowed to leave town.

So, don't we ever get to play?

In such stories, there's no need for the writer to interject wit. But don't despair. You'll have your chance. What a dreary world it would be if you didn't.

Here's Patrick Durkin, displaying plenty of attitude in an outdoor column for Midwest Features:

> Is this the greatest country in the world or what?
>
> First we put a man on the moon, then we invent or import cut-proof golf balls, push-button telephones and remote controls for Volkswagen-size TVs.
>
> Now, just when we think we've solved the world's problems and consider popping open a Miller, some genius invents a way to turn discarded tampon applicators into fishing lures!

It's a fairly funny premise, begging for playful treatment. Durkin could have played it relatively straight, cutting all the way down to "Some genius has invented a way to turn discarded tampon applicators into fishing lures" for his lead. But part of the fun here is the way Durkin introduces the subject, providing a satirical tone and a context of other technological achievements of questionable long-term value. Just as we read Dave Barry, Andy Rooney and Erma Bombeck more for how they say than for what they say, Durkin's attitude here becomes an integral part of the story.

I'm no Dave, Andy or Erma, but I took an approach similar to Durkin's to introduce a chapter on getting off the Interstate and rambling on the blue roads for a book I wrote on small towns in Wisconsin:

> It's hard to imagine life before word processing, the microwave oven, disposable diapers, and talking Barbie Dolls. We take our technological advances for granted.
>
> Surely those four lanes of concrete convenience called Inter-

states have always existed, enabling us to zip from Madison to Milwaukee or Janesville to Eau Claire without even slowing down.

Not so, of course. There was a time, back when television was just a rumor in many of our homes, when hardy pioneers made rigorous treks to distant places on winding roads that actually passed through towns and around farms.

The old roads are still there. . . .

"I" don't appear anywhere in this lead. But my attitude surely does.

Alex Witchel doesn't use the "I" word lead for his profile of actor Mickey Rooney for *The New York Times*. But his attitude shows:

Let everyone else in the world spend time and money trying to free his inner child. Mickey Rooney's is already free. You might even say it needs a spanking.

Tom Flaherty used to cover the Brewers baseball team for the *Milwaukee Journal*. That means 162 game stories a season (assuming the team doesn't make the playoffs, a safe assumption in recent years), 162 color stories, and 162 "notes" columns. Not all 162 games were scintillating (or perhaps even worth writing about). Sometimes Flaherty allowed a bit of attitude to seep into his reports, perhaps to refresh himself as much as his readers.

He began a game story from the depths of a Brewer batting slump, for example, with this twisted cliché: "Things were so quiet in the Brewer clubhouse last night, you could hear a batting average drop."

Okay. Maybe "seep" isn't quite the right word. Maybe "spew" serves better.

On "Cushion Night," fans vented their frustrations with the team by hurling their gifts onto the field. Flaherty began his notes column with this observation: "Fortunately, it wasn't Bowling Ball Night." That's attitude, and it's fun. If someone had been killed by a flying cushion, the humor would have been out of place. Had Flaherty been covering an execution instead of a ball game, ditto. But this is baseball, and it's supposed to be fun.

Paul Daugherty let attitude hang out all over the page in his profile of professional football analyst John Madden for the *Cincinnati Post*:

I love John Madden. I would listen to John Madden analyze a traffic jam. I would watch him if he were covering the national championship finals of the Scholastic Aptitude Test. If I'd thought of it, I'd have had Madden do the color at my brother's divorce.

That's attitude. I don't even agree with it, not being a big John Madden fan, but I don't want to analyze it. I just wish I'd written it.

CHAPTER FIVE

Above All Else, Be Clear

I awoke one morning to the cooing of the reporter on National Public Radio, following up on the earthquake that had recently rocked San Francisco.

"The committee will have to prepare an estimate," she told me, "of how much it will cost to repair the damage by next Monday."

Still mostly asleep and easily addled, I foolishly assumed she meant what she said. It will probably cost a lot, I thought, to get all that damage cleaned up by next Monday.

That's not what she meant, of course. She meant that the committee had to prepare the estimate by next Monday. "By next Monday" had apparently gotten up from its rightful place at the beginning of the sentence, or snuggled in after "estimate," and wandered to the end of the line, where it had no business being.

So, what's the harm? I figured out what she meant, and I even got a little chuckle to begin my day. But I did have to work at it, if only a little, and I also figured that whoever wrote the copy must be pretty sloppy to let such a shoddy piece of work slip through. (I can be a tad judgmental first thing in the morning.) And once you lose faith, even in a relatively small thing, you might just lose trust in all things. (Was there really an earthquake?)

Word order doesn't matter? Consider the following sentence: "I hit him in the eye yesterday."

Insert the word "only" anywhere you like and read the result. Now pick up your "only" and set it down somewhere else and read your new creation. You won't try to tell me that,

"I hit only him in the eye yesterday,"

for example, means roughly the same thing as,

"I hit him in the eye only yesterday,"

or

"I only hit him in the eye yesterday,"

or even

"I hit him in the only eye yesterday,"

or any other combination you could create by shifting that one little "only."

Of course word order matters. You have to put the "only" precisely where you want it, and no place else, so your reader will get the one and only meaning you intended, without having to guess at it (and without being handed a laugh at your expense).

Even the tiniest of elements, the period and the comma, can make a difference. Punctuate the following:

woman without her man is helpless

Sexist, you say? Then you rendered it this way:

Woman, without her man, is helpless.

But what if you had done this instead:

Woman. Without her, man is helpless.

If you can't teach, administrate

I hit this patch of fog while trying to get into a memo from a school administrator:

It is necessary that schools and school districts emphasize the importance of imparting to students the skills and attitudes which are the underpinnings of a comfortable, confident, successful producer of all forms of written matter, including prose, poetry, and practical narrative, descriptive and interrogatory writing (e.g. letters, applications, requests for information, reports, etc.).

Pretty awful, isn't it? Look up the word "bloviation," and you'll probably find a picture of the pompous idiot who wrote this, or at least his near kin.

When my head finally cleared, I figured out he was probably trying to say, "Schools should teach kids to write well." So why didn't he? He was probably scared that if he put it plainly, we might actually understand him (and ask, "So why aren't you doing it?").

Now imagine that you happened upon this dense patch, not in a bureaucratic memo, where you would probably expect such obstacles, but in your morning newspaper as the lead to an article on education. Would you be willing to take the time and make the effort to translate? Would you read on, expecting more of the same? I'll bet not. I'll bet you'd take an angry sip of coffee and turn the page, looking for something written in English.

You must always be clear. (Or, put in educationalese, "It is necessary that you always impart clarity.") You must be especially clear in the lead, where the reader decides whether to join you or pass you by. You must know exactly what you want to say, and then you must have the courage to say it exactly.

This writer (for *The New York Times*, no less) probably knew exactly what he meant to say with this lead. Do you?

> Congress is moving toward overturning a Supreme Court ruling that made it easier to restrict religious practices that violate state or Federal laws.

Leave "moving toward" go. I have no idea what it means (I can imagine a surly Congress slinking down a darkened hallway toward a cowering Supreme Court ruling), but am willing to chalk it up to journalistic convention of the sort that leaves a patient in "guarded condition" (which conjures for me the image of a cop, gun at the ready, standing in the hallway outside the hospital room).

Let's get to the gist. Congress is considering overturning (reversing, nullifying) a ruling that makes it easier to make it harder to perform religious observances that break laws. So, if I want to set up a nativity scene in a public park or pop peyote as part of a religious rite, is Congress going to help me or hurt me? Takes a bit of figuring, doesn't it? The ruling made it easier to restrict. Congress will make it harder to restrict, making it easier to pop the peyote. Phew! That's just too much work. In Clarke Stallworth's terms, the "get" is too low, the "cost" too high. Most readers aren't going to pay.

Forgetting to pass "Go"

By the time you begin writing an article or chapter, you probably know how it will end. That may be the second major difference between fiction and nonfiction (the primary difference being, of course, that in nonfiction, you're not supposed to make the stuff up). Although the task of forming ideas and images into words on paper is basically the same either way, the fictionist is perhaps more artist (and thus doesn't necessarily know what she'll have when she's finished), the journalist more artisan (who knows what the pot is supposed to look like when it comes out of the kiln).

But there's a potential danger in knowing where you're going and having at least a rough idea of how you intend to get there. You may skip a step or two, leaving your poor reader—who doesn't have a copy of the map, remember—lost at the crossroads.

That may have been the problem in this lead from a Michigan daily (with the name of the subject changed):

> The owner of Pozzo's Pizza, where the remains of a puppy were found in the restaurant's freezer, pleaded guilty Tuesday in Kalamazoo District Court to having too many dogs on his restaurant property.

At least one too many, certainly.

We later learn that the owner (I'd love to use his name, since it provides a great natural pun, but I must refrain) pleaded no contest to the charge of having "unsanitary conditions" at his pizzeria. The place had previously been closed because of health violations. Okay, so the problem isn't just "too many dogs" on the property. But the lead leaps over twenty-nine dogs and a couple of cats before it gets to the little matter of the puppy in the freezer.

We need to make sure we take the reader along with us when we begin negotiating a story with lots of curves and switchbacks.

Losing the numbers game

Here's another befuddlement, from the health pages of *The New York Times*:

> While approximately 52 million adults in the United States— more than one in four—suffer from a mental disorder at some point during a year, only 28 percent of them seek help, according to the most comprehensive study of the nation's mental health ever conducted.

Numbers are always tough. Is it 28 percent of adults in the United States, or 28 percent of the "more than one in four"? After not much reflection, we can be fairly certain it's the latter. So how much is one-fourth of one-fourth? While we're pondering that, we're missing the point—that a lot of us suffer from a mental disorder but don't seek help. The numbers must wait until we've expressed the significance.

The infamous "mil rate" provides a yearly headache for any reporter (to say nothing of the headaches it produces in local taxpayers). Mil-rate stories bloom like the crocus in spring, and most lead with something along the lines of:

> The Common Council has set this year's mil rate at $1.13.

Terrific. But ask the reader what a mil rate is, and you'll get a blank stare or a bad guess. Readers don't know a mil rate from an old mill stream.

We must do a little work here, so the reader doesn't have to.

First, we must define the term. "The mil rate is the amount of tax a property owner pays for each $1,000 worth of assessed valuation of the property." Then we need to put this year's rate into meaningful context. "That's an increase of $.19 or 16.8 percent over last year's rate. That compares to a rate of $.68 in neighboring Burlington County." And we must translate the statistic into its immediate significance for the reader:

> If your home was assessed at $50,000, you'll pay $56.50;
> if your home was assessed at $60,000, you'll pay $67.80; . . .

(I want to live in this county, don't you?)

Couldn't the reader multiply 50 times $1.13? Sure. And she might even do it. But she shouldn't have to. She should be able to grasp the significance of our words in the time it used to take Lawrence Welk to deliver the downbeat. If your lead can't pass the "And-a one and-a two" test, you need to rewrite it.

And finally, we must tell the reader what the Common Council will be spending our money on (the "what do I get?" to go along with the "how much will it cost me?").

The history of the world in a single sentence

Sometimes we run into clarity problems from trying to say too much too soon. If the lead is all important, after all, we're tempted to say all the important stuff in the lead. But that's a lot like talking faster and more softly on discovering that your listener doesn't understand English.

Remember that admirable story about the endangered yew tree? The story has a happy environmental ending. But the lead on the AP story suffers from a slight case of Faulkneritis, the attempt to say it all in the first sentence or two:

> The company that produces Taxol, the anti-cancer drug derived from the bark of rare Pacific yew trees that grow in Federal

forests here in Oregon and in Washington State, says it has made such rapid progress in synthetic production of the drug that it can stop harvesting the trees immediately.

Here's another example of Faulkneritis, from an Illinois newspaper, with the names changed to protect innocent and guilty alike:

> On August 31st, the same day authorities arraigned Beauregard Longhorn Culbertson, who was charged with shooting George Ratterree and Carla Wolfgang during the March 25th robbery in Sardinia, the Federal Drug Enforcement Agency released a legal notice stating that Federal Drug Agents had seized the $130,000 home where the shooting had occurred.

All we need is the mil rate on that $130,000 home to totally fog the mirror.

Here's an even more harried pileup of *who's* and *which's* from a Minnesota weekly:

> On January 15, eleven state representatives who are members of the Environment and Natural Resource Committee, which is chaired by Victoria Mallard of Duluth, met in Babbitt as part of the Legislature's mini session on the Iron Range. They heard testimony from the Waste Management Board (WMB), which was created in 1980 to manage both hazardous and solid waste in Minnesota, and toured TireCycle and Whirl-Air Rubber Products, two new companies which are involved in the recycling of waste tires.

Not one mention of when Babbitt was founded, and by whom, and not one word on what sign of the zodiac Victoria Mallard was born under, but otherwise, we've pretty much got the whole story massed like a boulder squatting in the reader's path, preventing her from going any farther.

The William F. Buckley School of Vocabulary Enhancement

When I set out to be a writer, I put myself through the Funk & Lewis *30 Days to a More Powerful Vocabulary* crash course. It was great. I learned words like "pusillanimous" and other polysyllabic marvels. (Actually, I already knew "pusillanimous," it having been my father's favorite description of a Democrat, *any* Democrat.) But when I tried to use some of my new wonder words, I realized that it just didn't make good sense to use "conflagration," which few would understand (unless they were fellow Funk & Lewis graduates), when "fire" would serve so much better—assuming, of course, that I wanted to communicate and not to flex and strike a pose before the mirror.

A rich vocabulary gives us lots of choices, a good thing. It also helps us understand the William F. Buckleys of this world, so we won't be confounded or unduly impressed by anyone's show of linguistic dexterity. But taking up the cudgel of big words and beating your own poor reader with it? Never.

Do you suppose this writer for *Editor & Publisher* was showing off just a bit?

> After a long illness — begun with the exodus of downtown businesses, exacerbated by competition and finalized by recession — the Holyoke, Mass. *Transcript-Telegram* ended 110 years as a daily newspaper on Jan. 21 by transforming into four weeklies.

The poor paper might have choked on its own obituary. "Exacerbated"? Have mercy.

When lame ducks soar like missles

As we saw in the last chapter, we can also get all tangled up in language, image and allusion, getting in the way of the meaning instead of conveying it. Here's an example from the *Boston Globe*:

> Most presidents go to ground when they become lame ducks. Not George Bush. Defeat at the hands of Bill Clinton seemed to energize him. Becoming a rara avis in the lame duck catalog, Bush spent his last days in office winging as high as a Tomahawk missile.

I'm just not real sure what a "rara avis in the lame duck catalog" might be. And trying to visualize a lame duck transmogrifying or otherwise metamorphosing into a Tomahawk missile simply exacerbates my muddle.

The next paragraph contains a Latin pun ("pax" for "pox") and references to "Rough Rider testosterone" and the Marx Brothers, with a pun on "lame duck" soup. The third paragraph starts with Bush stomping "a warpath to the finish line."

This writer seems to have begun with the question, "What's the most clever way to say it?" Or perhaps the challenge was, "What's the most impressive way to say it?" or "What's the most creative or original way to say it?" These are the wrong questions. You must always begin with this question and no other: *"What's the most clear, direct way to say it?"*

Never sacrifice clarity for cleverness.

Never write to impress.

We would do well, here, to take a cue from one of the most powerful orators of the day, the Reverend Jesse Jackson. Speaking to the Democratic National Convention in 1988, Jackson described the plight of the working poor. He didn't hide behind statistics, pile up metaphors, or use pretty language. He used clear, direct language to talk about real people doing real things.

> Most poor people are not on welfare. They work every day. They take the early bus. . . . They care for other people's babies and they can't watch their own. They cook other people's food and carry leftovers home. . . .
>
> They are janitors running the buffing machines. They are nurses and orderlies wiping the bodies of the sick. A loaf of bread is no cheaper for them than it is for the doctor. . . . They change beds in the hotels. Sweep our streets. Clean the schools for our children. They're called lazy, but they work every day. . . .
>
> No job is beneath them. And yet when they get sick, they cannot afford to lie in the bed they've made up every day.

Not an exacerbated or a rara avis in the bunch.

Agree or disagree, accuse Jackson of oversimplification or hail him as a saint. Whatever you do, you'll have understood what he was saying.

And that's the point.

CHAPTER SIX

Beginning Anywhere But at the Beginning

Remember Ted Baxter, the blowhard, blow-dried television news anchor on the old *Mary Tyler Moore Show*? As played by actor Ted Knight, Baxter was full of himself and very little else. He seized on any chance to talk about himself, and when he did, he always began at the beginning: "It all began at a little radio station in. . . ."

In a way, Baxter was right. When the subject is human beings in all their wondrous complexity and contrariness, there is no simple way to describe them. If you *really* want to know a person, you must start at the beginning. Ken Kesey knew this when he crafted his second novel, *Sometimes a Great Notion*. At the beginning of the novel, which is actually about five minutes away from the end of the plot, a minor character asks a seemingly simple question: "Why have the Stamper brothers insisted on defying a town and a labor union by trying to bring a load of logs to market?" The story takes off on a long, circular journey, back several generations of Stampers to the western migration from Kansas to Oregon, then up through Hank Stamper's tempestuous relationship with brother Leland, and finally back to the present moment.

And, 600 pages of marvelous stream-of-consciousness narration later, we still can't put an easy answer to the original question.

This sort of meticulous tracking down of prime causes is, of course, totally inappropriate in answer to a casual "How're you doin'?" Just try Baxter's start-at-the-beginning and include-every-detail technique the next time you meet someone at a social gathering.

"How're you doing?"

"Well, when I was born, in St. Luke's Hospital, in Pasadena, California, I had a condition called pyloric stenosis. They had to operate when I was eleven days old. But then I was a fairly healthy baby until. . . ."

It's a lot like launching into the history of the watch when someone asks you for the time of day.

Here's an example of a lead that fails because the writer insists on starting at the very beginning. The headline seems to promise a good time:

Library Celebrates
30th Anniversary

But the lead delivers, not a party, but a plebiscite.

It was on April 18, 1959 that a referendum was passed establishing the Niles Public Library District as a tax supported library.

We could strengthen the language by getting rid of the passive voice and the "This is the place in which George Washington slept" circumlocution:

On April 18, 1959, the residents of Niles passed a referendum establishing the Niles Public Library District as a tax supported library.

But the essential problem remains. Even in more direct language, the lead fails to deliver on promises made.

The article contains a number of interesting tidbits, including:

- a survey showing that 61 percent of the residents used the library in the last year
- statistics indicating that library holdings include not only 158,000 books but almost 1,000 videotapes, over 1,000 cassettes, and over 500 computer software programs
- a listing of attractions during the anniversary celebration, including something called "Dr. Gesundheit's Clown Therapy Show."

The article concludes with an announcement of an essay contest.

Any of those items would have made a better lead, in my view, than that poor referendum. We could go with a "Your library — it isn't just books anymore" angle, perhaps listing a few of the more offbeat videotape and cassette titles available. We could interview a few of those 61 percent who use the library and get some sharp quotes for the lead. ("The library is my favorite place on all the earth.") I think I'd get on the phone to Dr. Gesundheit, find out exactly what "clown therapy" is all about, and perhaps lead with that.

There's no single "right" lead for this or any other story. But there are lots of possibilities. Even the rather prosaic second sentence of the first paragraph would have been a much better choice:

> To celebrate the library's 30th anniversary, a series of special programs and events will be held.

although we'd generate a bit more excitement by taking it out of passive voice:

> We'll celebrate the library's 30th anniversary with a series of special programs and events.

Dark and stormy observation #1: If you promise a party, don't deliver a referendum.

What's wrong with a little history? Nothing. Some folks will be fascinated by the background information. (These same folks might also be fascinated by a discussion of watchmaking through the ages.) For those folks, we could put the history lesson in a boxed sidebar story, easy to find for those who want it, easy to skip for those who don't. Or we could put it down toward the bottom of the story, with its own subhead, again so that the reader can choose to seek it out or skip it, according to need, desire and time.

But if we lead with an element that may be irrelevant to many and of little interest to most, we force the reader into a bad choice—wade through this material to get to the good stuff, or skip the whole article. Given this sort of all-or-nothing choice, many readers will choose nothing, and miss all that good information farther down in the story. They also won't show up at clown therapy or any of the other events, which was the real point of the article in the first place.

We must lead with something of potential interest or value to the reader. The more interest or value for the greatest number of readers, the better the lead. Sticking to chronological order— first the library was founded, and then it was built, and then it moved to its present location, and then—serves neither reader nor writer interests.

We find the same sort of problem with an otherwise marvelous feature for an employee newsletter, run under this rather intriguing headline:

Manager profile
From beer to brats, to bum to boss

This month our manager profile features Harry Bradshaw, Dry Department manager. Harry was born and raised in the Philadelphia, PA area . . .

We're twenty-one words into the lead, with no beer in sight, and no reason to want to read on. "It all began at a little radio station. . . ."

Why did the writer choose this approach? Because profiles for this newsletter have always begun with this formula: First give name. Then give title. Then give place of birth. Then tell what father and mother did. Then list schools. Then you'd better remember to wake the reader up. Fact is, the writer probably didn't choose at all. She just plugged the elements into the formula.

Those with enough determination to press through this rather unpromising lead will discover that Harry Bradshaw has led a fascinating work life. Among other singular achievements, he:

• served as a sausage taster. (He was like the canary in the mine shaft. If his eyes didn't glaze over after sampling the sausage, they figured the stuff was safe.)
• delivered cars around the country and hitchhiked back home.
• parked cars at Philadelphia Airport.

A good reporter would of course ask, "Did you ever park a car for any celebrities?"

Yeah. Harry Bradshaw, Dry Department manager, that friendly guy in the next cubicle, parked Muhammad Ali's car for him the night Ali lost to Joe Frazier. Harry Bradshaw is the only person in the universe who parked Muhammad Ali's car at the Philadelphia Airport as Ali prepared to meet his destiny against Joe Frazier in the ring.

Dark and stormy observation #2: A brush with greatness makes a great feature lead.

How is your subject different from anyone else in the world? If your lead answers that question, you've got a winner.

But Harry's personal life provides equally worthy contenders for the lead. His honeymoon trip with his bride, Mary Beth, was cut short when the van they were driving blew up sixty miles from Moose Jaw, Saskatchewan, Canada. I don't know about you, but I'd need a mighty good reason to pass up a chance to put an exploding honeymoon van in the lead, and I'll grab almost any pretext to use "Moose Jaw, Saskatchewan" there. (No reason. I just like the sound of it.)

Dark and stormy observation #3: If you have an excuse to put Moose Jaw in your lead, do it.

The writer obviously did a superior job of drawing stories from her subject and capturing them clearly and concisely. She just lost her nerve when it came time to pick one of those gems for the lead.

Every human being is different. Every lead should reflect that difference. People are worth more than a formula.

Has anyone ever succumbed after a cowardly battle?

At least Harry will live to compile more good stories and perhaps serve as the subject for another feature story. The subjects of formula obituaries aren't as lucky.

Lots of newspapers handle obituaries in the same sort of rote, formula manner as the "This month our profile features . . ." approach. The late-lamented dies after a brief illness or a courageous fight, is survived by, and will be buried out of . . . Send your donations to . . . Next.

The Guntersville, Alabama *Advertiser-Gleam* refuses to succumb to the easy formula. Each obit in the *Gleam* is a mini-profile, reflecting the life of its subject.

> Although she taught school nearly half a century, the most unusual thing about Mrs. Vivian Dollie Walls Clay was her love of baseball. She went to New York to see her favorite team, the Yankees. . . . and she saw Hank Aaron break Babe Ruth's home run record.

Developing that kind of detail takes more time and effort than the formula lead, but it's well worth it. Each obit gleams with the uniqueness of its subject, because the lead is specific and focused.

The Arkansas *Democrat Gazette* runs a feature obit every day capturing the essence of the subject, as with this effort by Wayne Jordan:

> C.R. Lederman, a private man, never did like crowds and stirring up hoopla over just anything. He preferred to be with a couple of good coon dogs in the Moro Bottoms on a crisp winter night than going to a movie or just sitting around.

Shots rang out!

If your story contains action, enter the story at the prime time—the moment of decision, of maximum tension, of peak significance. You'll let the reader know why she needs to read the rest of the story.

Peter Hecht's piece for the *Los Angeles Herald Examiner* on the vulnerability of convenience stores to robberies begins precisely at 2:10 A.M., as the night clerk at the North Hollywood 7-Eleven market comes "face to face with two men—and a blue-steel revolver."

> "Okay, sunshine," the gunman demanded. "Let's take a walk to the back room."

The clerk jumped over the counter. And ran.

Want to know what happens next? Of course. The clerk escaped, called police, and quit his job.

"I don't want you to talk to him," a manager at the store told Hecht. "I have enough trouble finding people to work this shift."

And with that telling quote, Hecht opens the story to the wider question of the relative safety, or lack thereof, of convenience store clerks in general.

Dark and stormy observation #4: Don't start with sociology. Start with a gun held to your victim's head.

A gripping Associated Press story, datelined Fairfax, Virginia, begins with a woman uttering a few simple words.

> "My name is Cathy," said the young woman in the hospital bed. The policeman trying to interview her about the traffic accident that left her face disfigured and killed four other people was stunned.
>
> In a tragic mixup, Cathy had been identified as one of the dead.

The writer begins, not at the beginning, with a report of the traffic accident, and not at the end, with the family's reaction, but at the turning point, when the mistake is first discovered.

Dark and stormy observation #5: Don't begin at the beginning. Begin when things start to get interesting.

Making the case for the leisurely lead

Lest we get hyper about all this need to come right to the point, let's take a look at a wonderful lead that wends its way slowly into its subject.

Jacquelyn Mitchard's column in a recent edition of the Sunday *Milwaukee Journal* carried this headline:

**3 tiny words
still carry
great weight**

But we don't find out what those three little words are until the sixth paragraph, 204 words into a 600-word column. Mitchard chats about folks' willingness to give her advice ("If advice were Velcro, I'd stick to all the chairs in my house"), about the two basic kinds of advice ("the kind that does the adviser good from giving it, and the kind that does you good from getting it" — most falling into the first category), and about the first good piece of advice she ever got, from Patty Bavone, in the sixth grade: "Whether you want your hair to turn up at the ends or under at the ends, always roll it under on the roller."

Mitchard then spends a paragraph lamenting the passage of the hair style known as "the flip" ("Marilyn Quayle . . . was its last champion").

After all this, Mitchard at last comes to those three little words of good advice alluded to in the headline and given her by her grandmother: "Sleep on it."

"Almost everything," she decides, "really does look better in the morning."

Why all the meandering? Because it's fun, and because this is a column in a Sunday newspaper, designed to entertain as well as to inform.

Dark and stormy observation #6: You don't necessarily have to be important from the first word, but you'd better start having fun right away.

Giving your lead the "What happens next?" test

The wisdom to know where to begin may simply present itself to you as you gather your material and bring it to the writing table. But often you'll have to discover the telling moment by writing your way into it. Give your approach this test: If you were telling the story to a neighbor, where would you begin (with "I got up at 5:15 and fixed myself a big bowl of Quaker Oat Squares, with bananas and milk . . . " or "I saw a guy get hit by a car on my way to work")? Which lead, if told to a neighbor or friend, would evoke an immediate, "Well, what happens next?" That's the lead you want.

Final dark and stormy observation: Don't lead with Oat Squares. Lead with traffic accidents.

CHAPTER SEVEN

Avoiding the Trite and True and the Pernicious Passive

W̲hat do Victoria McGlothren, Dave Carlson, Jane Tompkins, Ron Powers and Anna Quindlen have in common?

At least three things, actually. They're all fine nonfiction writers. You'll meet them all in this book. And I'll bet none of them would lead with something as stale and overused as "What do . . . have in common?"

I took a chance there, didn't I, leading a chapter on bad leads with what I consider to be a bad lead? After six chapters together, I'm hoping you trust me enough to give me the benefit of the doubt for a line or two. But I wouldn't count on that sort of goodwill with a stranger, a reader browsing through a magazine or grazing the shelves at the bookstore.

Why you should avoid clichés like the plague

"Raining cats and dogs" probably packed quite a sensual punch the first few times you heard it. That would be some rain, after all, with the screeching of an angry alley cat and the clawing of a frightened schnauzer or a rabid Doberman. But precisely because it was so evocative, the poor phrase got used and used and used. Now, when you hear it, you don't hear any screeching or feel any clawing. You probably don't even register any rain.

We can wear out approaches just as surely as we can overuse words and phrases. My "have in common" lead isn't bad so much as it's a good format that has been loved to death. The reader we're trying hard to woo may be so familiar with the format, she'll miss the specific application that's supposed to catch her attention and guide her into the body of the material. An alarm may go off in her head, warning her that she's read this all before someplace.

What do Muhammad Ali, Henry Kissinger and Sylvester Stallone have in common? I haven't the foggiest notion, and I certainly don't want to try to make something up.

Other overused formats? Well, according to the dictionary, "overuse" means "to use excessively," and "excessively" means "greater than what is necessary or normal, too much," and all that means we probably shouldn't lead with a dictionary definition, either, because that approach has surely been done to death.

Closely akin to the dictionary definition and its strong rival in ability to make a reader's eyes glaze over, we find the yawner, "[insert theme word here] is not a word to be found in [insert subject's name here] vocabulary," as in "Retirement is not a word that could be found in Gertrude Pulvermacher's vocabulary." Either Gertrude has a mighty small vocabulary, or the writer of her profile just hasn't worked hard enough to come up with an original approach. I'll bet Gertrude knows what retirement means; she just doesn't want to do it. Better to say, "Gertrude Pulvermacher has no intention of retiring" and get to the juice.

Here's another starter on the all-time all-trite lead team:

> It was literally standing room only at the Beymer City Council meeting Monday night as about 50 people jammed the Village Hall to protest a record budget.

Apparently, the joint was so crowded, folks had to stand up literally, which must be in some way different than having to stand up figuratively. Let's yank "literally." The usage is correct here but unnecessary.

And watch out any time you use "literally." We've seen it misused in print so often—precisely when the writer means the opposite but is straining for importance—we're apt to plug it in when we shouldn't, as in:

> The Beymer Village Hall was literally packed to the rafters last night as approximately 50 people turned out to protest . . .

I'll bet the hall *wasn't* packed to the rafters, literally, figuratively or any other way. I'll bet it was just very crowded. (If it were packed to the rafters, the fire marshal must not have been among the fifty in the crowd.)

But even without the offending "literally," our original example is pretty tepid stuff, relying as it does on the tired "standing room only" cliché stolen from theater parlance.

The failure of a cliché is especially resounding when we inject the phrase precisely because we want to heighten the drama. Instead of simply handing down a verdict, for example, the writer could have the judge "seal the fate" of the defendant. Could, but shouldn't.

But what do we do when the judge really *did* seal the verdict, as with this Associated Press report datelined Detroit:

> Former Detroit police officer Robert Lessnau, charged with assault in the beating death of Malice Green, sat unmoved as the judge sealed his fate in a white envelope.
>
> The verdict will remain sealed until jurors reach decisions in the second-degree murder cases against. . . .

Even here, I vote to avoid the tired combination of words and simply have Judge George Crockett III seal the verdict, not the fate.

The hit movie or book of the day can spawn an instant cliché lead, as when "Everything you always wanted to know about sex . . . but were afraid to ask" hit public consciousness years back and uncorked a flood of fill-in-the-blanks imitations, such as:

> Everything you always wanted to know about lead writing but were afraid to ask.

Pretty catchy, eh? It's inappropriate as well as trite. Nobody's afraid to ask about lead writing. But they probably won't ask much of an article or chapter title that begins in such an unpromising way.

Sail on, oh cliché of state . . .

How to correct a cliché? We could strain and struggle for a better figure of speech or turn of phrase:

> The Beymer Village Hall was loaded to the gunnels . . .

What's that? You don't know what a "gunnel" is? Okay. How about,

> The Beymer Village Hall was loaded to the gunwales . . .

Oh, come on. You don't know that the "gunwale" is the upper edge of the side of the ship? Then I guess the image won't work. How about,

> was crammed tighter than a tick . . .
> was like 10 pounds of sausage in a five-pound skin . . .
> looked like a department store the day before Christmas . . .

Given enough time, I might actually come up with an image worth hanging onto (although I certainly haven't done so yet). More likely, I'm just going to get in the way, inserting my cleverness—or attempt at cleverness—between the reader and the story. I've simply delayed her getting to the point.

The best way to get rid of the cliché usually involves grabbing an ax, taking a good, swift swing, and lopping it off cleanly.

> Over 50 people turned out last night to protest . . .

When in doubt, just chop it out.

We don't care where or when until we know what

The time/date/place lead is probably the most unpromising cliché lead of all, but it has cluttered the pages of newspapers and newsletters for years.

> On February 15, 1993, at 9:00 P.M. EST, a speech was given by President Bill Clinton in the Oval Office of the White House.

And a good time was had by all.

Of all the things we could say about a speech from the President of the United States, or a presidential candidate, or the lunchtime speaker at the local Rotary Club, time, date and place are surely among the least important, especially once the speech is over. What did the President say? How will what he said affect the reader? Oh, but we were getting to that in the second paragraph? Too bad. The reader might not get that far.

How about:

> The middle class won't be getting that promised tax cut, President Bill Clinton warned the nation last night.

Not great literature, but specific and to the point. The reader can choose to read more or move on, based on a clear understanding of what the article is all about. Even if she chooses to move on, she'll have the essence of Clinton's remarks, gathered in the time it took Lawrence Welk to jump-start the Champagne Music Makers.

To avoid the stale time/date/place lead, you must make an often difficult and always subjective decision: What is this article really all about? Making this decision makes for good leads. Failing to do so makes for weak leads that fail to offer a reason for reading on.

To avoid any sort of trite and true lead, we must often do as creativity guru Roger von Oech suggests and "reject the first right answer." The cliché will come readily to mind precisely because we've read it often before. But if the solution works on a variety of problems, it probably doesn't work especially well for any of them.

If you've let the deadline get too close and the desperation too high, or if you simply don't feel like working hard, you might be tempted to grasp at that vague "right" answer the way a politician grasps at a public opinion poll. Unclasp the cliché, let it go, and move on to a more specific, and thus more effective, approach.

Why you must shun the pernicious passive

Pick any good lead — or any good sentence, for that matter — and I'll bet you find that the most important word in it isn't a noun, an adjective or an adverb. I'll bet a strong, active verb is carrying the bulk of the load.

In that bad speech lead example, the speech "was given" by President Clinton. That's the pernicious passive, further bogging down an already slow-moving lead. The second example, when President Clinton "warned" the nation, uses a much more active and engaging verb.

The verb "to be" does very little work. That's why the passive voice should be shunned. What's that? Sorry. We should *shun* passive voice — or *dump* it, or *obliterate* it, and instead use active voice and active verbs.

> The Tomah Community Orchestra *was conducted* by Lyda Lanier.

No high crimes committed. It's just better this way:

> Lyda Lanier *conducted* the Tomah Community Orchestra.

Use of the passive presents an even larger obstacle for the reader if we couple it with a nonexistent or vague noun, as in this local news report:

> A second legal opinion has been rendered concerning the most recent petition submitted to city hall in opposition to the construction or purchase of a new municipal building.

We're twenty-eight words into the article, and we don't have any idea what that opinion might be. We only know that the darn thing has been "rendered." (I thought that's what Oscar Mayer did to pork.)

Any reader determined and tenacious enough to plug on will eventually find out that the petition was no good because the folks who wrote it didn't first submit the whole business to a vote. Oh.

The passive proves especially ineffective when it obscures meaning, as in this example:

> Children playing with fire is thought to be the cause of a blaze that completely destroyed a house which was owned by . . .

> That is what the occupant told local fire department officials

We've got a real mess here. The passive does an especially large disservice; it's not only wordy, but it disguises the lack of a key bit of information, namely who did the speculating as to the cause of the fire. Let's strip out the passive and another small patch of useless words ("which was"):

> Children playing with fire may have caused a blaze that completely destroyed a house owned by . . .

Better, surely, because it's crisper. But we've still introduced a conclusion without telling the reader who did the concluding. We have two options:

> Fire completely destroyed a house owned by . . .
> (We'll deal with probable cause in the next sentence.)

or

> An occupant told local fire department officials that children may have caused the blaze that completely destroyed . . .

Since I don't much care for leading a sentence with "occupant" (sort of a junk-mail lead), I'd go with the first option.

And while we're on the subject of emphasis, we need to rid ourselves of one final clump of potentially evasive words before moving on to the happier subject of achieving brilliant leads.

What's the hold-up here?

> Dane County Executive Rick Phelps announced Tuesday that director of the Dane County Department of Human Services, Carol Lobes, will resign his office effective April 30, 1993 to become director of the Wisconsin Clearinghouse.

Same thing that's wrong here:

> President Bill Clinton announced Tuesday that Gov. Tommy Thompson was appointed to the National Governors' Association Task Force on Welfare Reform.

Nonfiction writers have to attribute statements to their sources. But putting the source first emphasizes the messenger over the message. The messenger is important, yes, especially if he or she carries a big title. But the first story is rightly about a resignation, the second about an appointment, not an announcement.

> Carol Lobes will resign as director of the Dane County Depart-

ment of Human Services, effective April 30, 1993, to become director of the Wisconsin Clearinghouse, according to Dane County Executive Rick Phelps.

Same information, different order, and thus different emphasis. Decide what the story's really about, and then say so, in fresh, active language.

We've slogged our way through the mire of cliché and passive leads. Now we're ready to soar into loftier leads, beginning in the next chapter with the quote lead.

CHAPTER EIGHT

Using Fiction Techniques in Your Nonfiction Lead: Part One

"*L*earning to write is learning who you are."
I began my profile of novelist Ben Logan (*The Land Remembers, The Empty Meadow*) for my newsletter, *Creativity Connection*, with this Loganism, and followed it immediately with another Logan quote: "The job is to get in touch with those undercurrents in yourself."

Very few plays have a narrator. (Thornton Wilder's *Our Town* is a notable exception.) The curtain rises, and a character begins to speak. A short story or novel could have a narrator, but often the story begins with dialogue. Fiction writers plunge the reader directly into the action by letting their characters speak for themselves.

What works in fiction can work in your nonfiction, too. Words straight from your "character's" mouth introduce the person as well as the subject and slant of the article. They do, that is, if you choose the opening quote carefully.

My profile of Frank Farley, the psychologist who developed the "Type-T" theory of the risk-taking personality, began with this quote from my source: "If you can't explain your theory to your barkeep, it stands no chance."

I wanted to snag the reader's attention and to introduce Farley as a straight-talker, not at all the obtuse theoretician a "professor" label might have conjured up for some wary readers.

After a long series of interviews with master photographer Vern Arendt, a colorful and gifted speaker, I found my lead in a quote that exemplified Vern's approach to his craft and his "can-do" approach to life: "Make a picture. Don't take a picture."

Here are a few of the other quote leads I've used:

"A writer is always a prisoner of his story." — novelist George V. Higgins.

"If you only write the story that is planned, you'll miss the story that is discovered." — novelist and short story writer Ellen Hunnicutt.

"There's never been a better time to be a writer, teetering economy notwithstanding." — television screenwriter Delle Chatman.

"Throw out the rules. Rules restrict. There are no laws or rules. The only thing is 'Does it work?' " — print designer Jan White.

"Resist the temptation to imitate." — creativity guru Sidney X. Shore.

My only real contribution was to let the experts have the first word.

Lest you get the idea that I'm the inventor and sole practitioner of the marvelous technique of using a quote for the lead, here's Glen Mathison, leading his coverage of a speech by journalist Seymour Hersh for the *Wisconsin State Journal*:

> "If the president of the United States wants to lie to the press and the American people, he can get away with it."

That's a lot better than "Seymour Hersh talked about the press and society last night," wouldn't you say?

What better way to lead a profile of the editor of *Bartlett's Familiar Quotations* than with an unfamiliar but intriguing quote. Christine Terp leads her profile for the *Christian Science Monitor* with this marvelous bit of whimsy, straight from the editor's mouth:

> "I couldn't live without my *Bartlett's*," said Emily Morison Beck, fumbling through a spanking-new copy. "I have to have an upstairs *Bartlett's* and a downstairs *Bartlett's*."

Economist Milt Rockmore created one of my all-time favorite quote leads (it almost made the Lead Hall of Fame coming up in a couple of chapters) with this stunner:

> "No no no no no no no no no no no no no no no no no yes."
> That's the way Tom Jackson, co-author of *The Hidden Job Market*, describes the job hunt in America today.

Sure, Rockmore could have led with something more prosaic, along the lines of, "Finding a job in America today is pretty tough" or even "You may have to hear 17 'no's' before you finally get to a 'yes.' " But all those little "no's" stretching across the column grab attention and rouse curiosity.

Gary Rummler uses a variation on the quote lead to great effect in a story in the *Milwaukee Journal* urging attendance at a reading at a local bookstore:

> "At eight in the morning Samuel Taylor was eating eggs. There were three of them, sunny-side up, the yolks softly set. He had cut them up, and when he slid pieces of the slick whites into his mouth, yolk ran down his chin. He was making a mess, but he did not care. . . ."

Read that out loud. It's fun.

If you want someone else to read it and more from the same book—be at the Harry W. Schwartz Bookshop. . . .

An offbeat and unexpected quote makes for an especially good lead. Gwen Ifill followed Bill Clinton around the golf course at Edgartown, Massachusetts, perhaps just waiting for something this good to put at the top of her President-on-vacation story for *The New York Times*:

> "Whoa, mama, stay up!"

This was the President of the United States speaking, and he was addressing a pockmarked white ball that he had sent sailing on a long drive toward the right.

Veteran writers learn to detect a good quote lead the moment it leaves the source's mouth. A group of editors and publishers assembled one afternoon in Reston, Virginia, after a stimulating day of workshops, to watch then-President Ronald Reagan defend himself at a press conference during the Iran-Contra arms-for-hostages controversy. After the usual sparring, a reporter asked Reagan if, in retrospect, he would do anything differently in his handling of the affair.

After delivering one of his marvelous "Wells," Reagan said, "I would not go down that road again."

Immediately, one of the editors watching in Reston said, "There's the lead."

Several heads nodded in agreement. The consensus among this group of publishing pros was clear.

The next morning, *The New York Times* account of the speech began with, "I would not go down that road again."

Sometimes the quote needs a setup

Finding a good quote lead is seldom that easy. And sometimes the good quote isn't easy for the reader to get without some help. You may need to prepare the reader before turning your source loose on her.

Putting your source's thoughts into your own words is called a *para-*

phrase or *indirect quote*. A paraphrase can make a fine lead, especially when you follow it with a direct quote, as I did in the lead for a profile in *Creativity Connection*:

> Writing a novel is like night-driving, according to best-selling novelist Elmore Leonard.
> "You can only see a little way ahead of you," Leonard notes, "but you can make the whole trip that way."

I also used paraphrase for this profile lead:

> You don't have to be an expert in order to write a review, according to John Kovalic, film, music and restaurant critic for the *Wisconsin State Journal*.
> "Sometimes it's even preferable not to know much," Kovalic says. "You can ask stupid questions."

I worried over the lead for a profile of a former college basketball star accused of taking drugs. After brainstorming the possibilities, I decided on the direct approach with this setup and quote:

> If you want to know whether or not Larry Petty uses drugs, just ask him.
> "I love life too much to use drugs," he'll tell you.
> "I love my kids too much to hurt them that way."

Cartoonist Chuck Jones (he invented the Roadrunner and had a hand in raising Bugs Bunny to stardom) shows that he can write, too, in his autobiography, *Chuck Amuck*. He begins one of his chapters by setting up a quote:

> A dear uncle told me once, when I was deep in despair at some injustice by some bureaucrat, scholastic or familial, "Chuck, they can kill you, but they're not allowed to eat you."

If the quote you want to use is too long, too cumbersome, repetitive, meandering or digressive, you can capture the essence in your own words but incorporate a few words of direct quote for credibility and authenticity to create what's called a *partial quote*.

Just as you must always take care not to take a direct quote out of context or in any other way distort the speaker's intention, you must also be careful to capture both the substance and the spirit of the comments in your partial quote, as I tried to do for this profile lead for *Creativity Connection*:

> Stu Carlson calls it "living on the edge."
> Six days a week the *Milwaukee Sentinel* gives Carlson "that

little rectangle to fill" on the editorial page, and, six days a week, Carlson fills it with biting satire and cartoon commentary.

I used partial quote again for a profile of the first Native American woman to serve as a full-time photographer on a daily newspaper:

> Photojournalist Mary Annette Pember says she felt "an important burden" when the *Cincinnati Enquirer* sent her to take pictures of a 15-year-old recovering alcoholic and drug addict.
>
> "People are trusting you," she says. "You have to get it right. People are honoring you by letting you into their lives."

I didn't quite feel that I could unleash editor/critic/writing coach Rene Cappon on my unsuspecting readers without a partial quote preamble:

> A "fault line" runs through American newspapers, according to Associated Press general news editor Rene Cappon. He finds "an awful lot of gray" in the paper and not nearly enough "reader type stories." Reading most newspapers, he says, is "like having a series of small strokes."

Brackets, parentheses and dots

You can do a bit—but only a very small bit—of rearranging and rewriting within a direct quote.

If you need to insert a word or phrase to clarify a quote, put your addition in brackets, like this:

> "Slowly he raised it [the gun] and pointed it directly at the victim's head," according to Officer Jamison.

Don't use a parenthesis. The curved lines indicate that the source said those exact words, but in a parenthetical or offhanded way, and you could probably just as easily use commas:

> "Slowly he raised it (the gun) and pointed it directly at the victim's head," Officer Jamison added.

or

> "Slowly he raised it, the gun, and pointed it directly at the victim's head," Officer Jamison added.

If the quote is particularly murky, you may be tempted to use several sets of brackets:

> "Slowly he [Sandoval] raised it [the gun] and pointed it directly at the victim's [Oswald's] head."

Don't. The result is a choppy mess, and the reader may become suspicious, wondering why you had to monkey around with things that much. Instead, use a partial quote:

> Sandoval slowly raised the gun and "pointed it directly" at Oswald's head, according to Officer Jamison.

If you need to omit part of a direct quote, indicate the omission with three dots. Don't use a dash or other punctuation, and don't use three dots for anything else. Reserve those little dots for their intended function:

> "In the beginning God created the heaven and the earth . . . And God said, Let there be light, and there was light."

You must be sure that the omission doesn't change the meaning of the quote, of course, and here again, be careful about overusing the technique and thus rousing the reader's suspicions:

> "This movie is without a doubt the most . . . spectacular . . . dazzling . . . production . . . in the great tradition of . . . Cecil B. DeMille . . ."

Finally, if the source makes a grammar mistake, fix it.

The source said, "I didn't think they was ever going to get the job done."

You write, "I didn't think they was ever going to get the job done no how."

Just kidding. You really write, "I didn't think they were ever going to get the job done."

You don't write, "I didn't think they was [sic] ever going to get the job done." The word "sic" in brackets means "This person is an idiot, and I'm smarter than he is," which is not only not nice, but probably not true.

Did he say it then, or is he saying it now?

Tom Jackson *describes* the job market, Elmore Leonard *notes* that writing is like night-driving, and Rene Cappon *says* that newspapers are in a sorry gray state. Chuck Jones's dear old uncle *told* his young nephew the sage advice about cannibalism.

Why do some quotes get delivered in the present tense, others in the past?

In general, use the present tense for verbs of attribution when writing a profile or other feature material. Present tense helps create a sense of immediacy and the illusion that the source is speaking directly to the reader, right now. It's an event, not words on paper.

But if you set the quote in a particular place and time, as when covering a speech, use past tense.

I let Ellen Hunnicutt speak directly to the reader by using present tense throughout her profile:

> Creativity isn't an add-on, she *says*. "It's part of your original equipment." You have to believe that you can produce ideas as good as anybody else's, she *says*.

But I wrote about Ben Logan in the context of his speech to a convocation for the Council for Wisconsin Writers, so I used past tense all the way:

> "I have to allow myself to think wild thoughts . . . to cry at the typewriter," Logan *said*. "This has nothing to do with craft. Craft only gives us a way to respond to the feeling level," which is the "birthplace" of creation, Logan *said*.

If you begin in the present, stay there, unless you have a specific reason to shift. Same goes for the past. Your reader will assume that any change you make has a purpose. If you just lost track of tense, you'll confuse and inconvenience the reader and perhaps even annoy her.

"Get out of my life!" she cooed

Enough of "said" and "noted." How about an occasional "opined" or "expostulated"? Why can't the speaker "shriek," "holler" or "bellow," "whisper," "murmur" or "coo"?

She can, of course. You should find a verb that conveys the emotional tone of the utterance when you can. But use fancy verbs sparingly, as you would use perfume or seasoning. Never use a word simply to impress the reader. You want to keep the focus squarely on the subject, not on yourself and your cleverness or erudition.

You'll find a lot of "says," an occasional "notes," and some "according to" constructions in the work of a skillful writer. And to find them, you'll have to make a conscious effort to look for them. When used properly, verbs of attribution become invisible.

Be especially wary of the word "claim," as in: "I am totally innocent of any wrong doing in this matter," Elmo *claimed*. Do you believe Elmo? Probably not. "Claimed" implies that the speaker is lying.

Be careful, too, with mixing up "infer" and "imply." When your source means it, without saying it directly, she is implying. When you draw the conclusion from what she said, you are inferring.

And remember, your verb of attribution must refer to actual words coming out of an actual mouth. Your speaker cannot "smile," "burp," or "bark" words. She can say them with a smile, while burping, or in a tone of voice that suggests a bulldog announcing the presence of an intruder in the junkyard.

"How're you doin'?" asked he

Sometimes we do things with words on paper that we would never think of doing when we talk. Inverting the subject and the verb of attribution falls into this never-never land: "Publishing my first novel was the realization of a lifelong dream," *said Jane Collins.*

If we wouldn't say it that way when telling it to a friend, there's no reason to say it that way when writing it down. Use subject plus verb. Invert them only if you need to modify the subject: "Publishing my first novel was the realization of a lifelong dream," *said Jane Collins, president of the local chapter of Romance Writers of America.*

One final note about attribution: You may not need as much of it as you think.

Here's a chunk of my profile of Delle Chatman. I've italicized the attributions. Could you eliminate any without creating confusion?

> "Stories are the only place where people come unguarded and starving," *she says.* "Writers may be "the last leaders the nation will trust," *she adds.*
>
> Her storytelling comes from her belief that she has a unique reason for living, unique stories to tell, *Chatman says.* "You must feel that these are the stories you were born to write," *she adds,* "and if you don't write them, the world will be a colder, darker place."

In retrospect (always the most accurate spect there is), I'd trim both "she adds" attributions.

In this, as in all things, keep the comfort and convenience of the reader uppermost in your mind. If you can eliminate words, add a bracket, create a paraphrase, or in any other way sharpen the clarity of the writing, do so joyfully, knowing you've done your reader a good turn.

CHAPTER NINE

Using Fiction Techniques in Your Nonfiction Lead: Part Two

The car stops, backs up. Three riders get out.

And the reader wonders where we are and what's in store for us as we begin to read an article about tracking wolves in Wisconsin by Dave Carlson in the *Milwaukee Journal*.

> They walk cautiously up to the large tracks along a soft road in western Douglas County, as if the creature that made the tracks might be watching nearby.
>
> "They're the real McCoy," says Dick Thiel, Wisconsin's wolf biologist.
>
> "They're wolf tracks."

Carlson had a lot of options here. He could have led with a quote from Thiel concerning the wolf's ill-deserved reputation as an enemy of humankind. He could have started with a news hook, Thiel's planned survey of the wolf population. He could have gone with statistics about dwindling wolf herds.

Instead, he chose a narrative lead, creating nonfiction that reads like a short story to get us out of the office and onto the trail, tracking our prey.

Instead of simply leading with a key quote from the speech, writer Rick Lyman opened his story for Knight-Ridder with fiction-like description:

> The thin man with a thatch of straw-colored hair approached

the microphone with deliberation, his long, delicate fingers extended toward the podium.

"What has happened in this country with apartheid is not, as some would have you believe, just a policy experiment that failed," the young man said. "It was a moral failure, an injustice."

The audience of blacks and whites shot to its feet, cheering. A white man in the third row shook with sobs.

What's going on here? Isn't that sort of thing supposed to be confined to the pages of novels and short stories? Not at all. Although Lyman's description must be based on accurate rendering of precise observation, rather than on the imagination of the author, nonfiction writers like Lyman rely increasingly on narrative tools to tell their stories.

Judith Hooper and Dick Teresi used the same approach to begin the first chapter of *The 3-Pound Universe*, their brilliant book on brain research:

Watching the mauve shadows of dusk move across the sandstone cliffs, the traveler felt suddenly weak. The cries of circling birds filled him with unease, and he sensed a mysterious presence behind him. . . . The outer world disappeared; he could no longer remember his name or why he had set off for Damascus. As he fell to the ground a voice cried out, addressing him by name: 'Saul, Saul, why persecuteth thou me?' "

Saul will of course become the Apostle Paul and journey all over the known world. His conversion experience, told graphically, begins the reader's journey through the known world of brain research, in quest not of "brain" but of "mind" or consciousness. It's a marvelous beginning to a marvelous book and signals us that the authors will render oceans of scientific research in clear, compelling terms, using stories that engage as well as inform.

Research now supports what common sense has long known—that we like to have someone tell us stories. Frank Denton, editor of the *Wisconsin State Journal*, joined up with three researchers from the University of Wisconsin-Madison Journalism School to study the preferences of 1,000 readers of the *St. Petersburg Times*. They discovered that folks tended to shun traditional news stories written in "inverted pyramid" style—who, what, where, when and why jammed into the top of the story, with information rendered in descending order of importance. Instead, they preferred a "narrative" style, stories told as stories, with a beginning and an end.

Use anecdote as antidote to reader resistance

Jane Tompkins begins her fine chapter on Louis L'Amour, one of our best and most prolific western writers, not out on the range but with a short, purposeful narrative set in a social services center in Costa Mesa, California, where she worked as a file clerk. One day she noticed a man absorbed in a western novel. She asked the man if he had read any Louis L'Amour. He had, and was aware that the writer had recently died.

"Some people should live forever," Tompkins quotes the man as saying, and then she draws the significance of the little story:

> The reverence and respect his words conveyed, their spare eloquence and strength of conviction, reminded me of L'Amour's best writing and of the tough-it-out-against-all-odds philosophy his writing stood for.

Those words and the story that introduces them provide focus and theme for the chapter on L'Amour that follows. Indeed, Tompkins uses little stories throughout *West of Everything*, one reason why the book is as entertaining as it is illuminating.

Natalie Angier begins her *New York Times* profile of "the Joyce Carol Oates of science writing" with this capricious description:

> Stephen Jay Gould is in the cafeteria of the California Academy of Sciences, and he is about to try what generations of children have delighted in doing whenever they have been in a lunchroom: blow the wrapper from a drinking straw at the ceiling and make it stick.

When the wrapper fails to launch, Angier quotes Gould saying, ". . . they can't even make a decent wrapper. It's outrageous."

With this small incident, Angier has captured the essence of Gould as childlike experimenter and social critic. As with the use of quote leads, the key is not that you use an anecdote but that you use a *telling* anecdote, one that illuminates the theme of the entire piece.

New York Times columnist Robert Lipsyte uses anecdote to lead his profile of a high school teacher and coach:

> One day, Pablo Munoz, who wears a jacket and tie so his students will see that a teacher can take as much pride in his appearance as does a drug dealer, told one of his bilingual social studies classes about William Howard Taft.
>
> "You know, President Taft and I had something in common. We both went to Yale."
>
> There was a shocked silence until one student blurted:

"Uh, Mr. Munoz? You was really in jail?"

I used anecdotes often to lead my articles for business magazines, to get the reader involved, yes, but also because I didn't really know a whole lot about business and felt much more comfortable writing about people. Here's an example:

> Call it an ecological irony.
> When activists Carol and John Magee wanted to publish an environmental newsletter back in 1983, they had a tough time finding recycled paper to print on.
> Not wanting to kill trees while trying to help create an earth-friendly ethic, they tracked down paper sources and cut the recycled paper to newsletter size. When others came to them to buy paper, a business was born in the basement of the Magees' Lansing, Michigan home.

The anecdote must work as a stand-alone story, drawing the reader in because she has met interesting people and wants to know more about them. But the story must do more. It must introduce the subject, the theme, and the mood of the piece. My anecdote about the Magees and their environmentally friendly company, Earth Care Papers, focused not only on their convictions but on the somewhat capricious nature of their entry into business.

For a profile of another eco-activist, Gary Milhollin, I began with what I hoped would be a compelling moment:

> Gary Milhollin faced the members of the Congressional Subcommittee on Technology and National Security last summer and, with characteristic directness and intensity, let them have it.
> U.S. forces in Saudi Arabia are facing their own technology, he told them. "If war comes . . . the West will be forced to bomb its own citizens to destroy its own exports."

I didn't attend that subcommittee hearing. I relied on news accounts and Milhollin's recollections. But even though I hadn't been within one thousand miles of Washington, D.C. when Milhollin was giving his testimony, I wanted to put the reader into the room with him, sensing the urgency with which he approaches his life's work.

My colleague Jim Sparks told me a gentle little story as we were talking over an article on friendship we hoped to write for *Mature Outlook*. When I sat down to draft the piece, Jim's story kept coming back to me. I decided to lead with it:

> On a trip to Florida, Jim Sparks was sitting in a Tampa cafe

when the only other customer struck up an early-morning conversation with him.

"Three things I tell you," the 87-year-old man said. "It's important to get plenty of exercise. Second, keep busy. Don't just sit in front of a TV set. But most of all, keep up with friends."

Good advice, precisely the primary point of the article, rendered more effectively, I think, for having come from the mouth of a fellow in a Tampa cafe instead of from a couple of anonymous writers with university titles after their names.

I use the anecdotal lead approach often when writing about writing for writers. Here's my lead for a *Writer's Digest* article called "The Writing Life Begins at 40":

> A woman arrives at her first writing workshop, sets aside her walker and announces, "Now I'm going to do what I want to do."
>
> "At the age of 91, she had finally given herself permission to write," says her teacher, Lenore Coberly.

Of all the stories I gathered from late-blooming writers as I prepared for that article, the vivid image of the lady with the walker seemed to me to best exemplify the courage and determination the writer needs. Since I wanted to stress that it's never too late to get started, I chose a ninety-one-year-old to make the point.

I could have used this lead as an example of a quote lead with a setup. Categories overlap. It doesn't matter what bin you store the technique in, as long as you can get it out and use it when you need it. No matter what you call them, master the tools you need to make your points and involve your reader.

CHAPTER TEN

Playing—But Playing It Straight—With Your Reader

Your applicant may be better prepared for the job interview than you are.

I didn't want to insult my reader when I fired off that salvo to launch my article on hiring for *In Business*. But I did want to get her attention and alert her to the need to read on.

The *startling statement lead* surprises by offering an opinion or fact that contradicts conventional wisdom and reader expectation. The reader is looking for a fast ball, and you throw her a curve.

Florence Wesselius' career as an adult educator began in the back room of a bar.

Hardly what readers of a teachers' magazine are expecting. I tossed out another surprise in the second paragraph.

It reached a peak recently with her induction into the Southwestern Wisconsin Educators Hall of Fame.

First put the teacher in a bar. Then take her from the bar to the Hall of Fame. Enough dissonance there, I hoped, to move a marginally motivated reader into the body of the article.

Associated Press writer Tad Bartimus coupled contradictions to lead a profile carrying the dateline Silverton, Colorado:

Every time Lynn Watson goes to work, he puts his life on the line for $13 an hour and calls himself a happy man.

We don't usually associate risking your neck with bliss, so Bartimus has established tension. He amplifies that tension in the second paragraph:

> He is paid by people he doesn't know, to perform a service they take for granted, in a place where, by the laws of nature, they shouldn't be.

And that's about as far as you want to try to stretch a surprise. Bartimus then reveals that Watson works for the highway department, keeping one of the most dangerous sections of paved road in the country open during the winter blizzards that often hit the mountainous stretch between Silverton and Durango. The work satisfies Watson, despite obvious hardship, because he knows he's saving lives.

Sandra Sanchez develops an excellent startling statement lead for *USA TODAY* by calculating the implication of a series of statistics and putting it right at the top of her story:

> Women will need another 1,000 years to match the political and economic clout of men, says a new U.N. report.

Leads surprise by challenging our assumptions (women are making great progress) or by putting together two notions we wouldn't normally associate (danger/contentment). Sometimes the writer tries to create or heighten the surprise by withholding a vital piece of information from the reader. It's the lead writer's equivalent of hiding in the bushes, springing out and yelling "Boo!"

Here's a classic *delayed revelation* lead from the UPI:

> Honey's family wanted to make sure their 4-year-old never had to worry about money if they should go first, so they opened a $10,000 savings account for her.

What's that? You've already guessed which bush the writer is hiding behind? Then maybe this approach is a bit too "classic" (read "trite"). The next paragraph carries the punch line:

> Parents regularly open such accounts for their children. Honey is a cocker spaniel.

Yep. Yet another "dog/cat/hamster inherits a wad of money" story. Such a "surprise," if there is any, might be about as enjoyable as the surprise of having your dance partner step firmly on your foot.

But a variation on the theme just might work. Here's a dog of a different color from *Chicago Tribune* writer Blake Gumprecht:

He grew up around a tavern on Chicago's West Side and started drinking at an early age.

Then one day last November, while drunk, he was struck by a truck while crossing the street in front of a bar.

We skim through another paragraph of detail before learning that this particular story of alcoholism and redemption centers on a nine-month-old black-and-white puppy named Tramp.

Alcoholic or heiress, it's still a dog hiding out there in the bushes. And it's a risky approach, for at least three reasons. First, delayed revelation can rapidly become a cliché. The first time is a surprise. The second time may already be a bore.

Second, the reader may feel manipulated. You knew it was a dog all along. So why didn't you tell us?

If the trick works, your reader will forgive you. But delayed revelation isn't likely to work unless you let the editor in on the secret, which leads to the third potential danger, having the surprise revealed in a headline, photo or caption.

Apparently nobody told the rest of the staff that the alcoholic dog was supposed to remain anonymous for three paragraphs. In the newspaper where I spotted it, Gumprecht's effort carried the headline, "Sober Tramp repays debt" (the capital letter in "Tramp" tipping us off or at least giving us cause for suspicion), and the story ran next to a photo of the rehabilitated dog, captioned "a healthy Tramp."

The same sort of sabotage undermined an otherwise artful delayed-revelation lead by Andrew Linker in *Baseball America*, dateline Harrisburg, Pa.:

> The broadcast goes off on time with a bouncy introduction that sounds a little like Ed McMahon and a lot like "Saturday Night Live":
>
> "Now, liiiiiiive from Riverside Stadium, it's New Britain Red Sox baseball."
>
> The voice comes from New Britain (Eastern) color commentator Don Wardlow. He's smooth, a homespun storyteller like Dizzy Dean but without the mangled syntax.

Only three paragraphs later does Linker mention the jet-black Lab, Gizmo, sitting at Wardlow's feet, or the Braille typewriter on the counter in front of him. Wardlow is professional baseball's only blind announcer.

Which hardly came as a great surprise, since the story ran under the headline

Blind Broadcaster Gives
New Britain Games Color

One of the best delayed-revelation leads I ever read concerned a woman who could remember vividly the day the President of the United States was assassinated. We don't learn until the third or fourth paragraph that the President in the lead is William McKinley, not John F. Kennedy, as most of us would have assumed. But since the headline already told us that the subject of the profile was celebrating her 104th birthday, the delayed revelation comes across as contrived and loses all power.

Ah, but when it all works, delayed revelation can be such a joy, as with this bracing Associated Press cutie:

Icy plunge 'refreshing'
The entire membership of the Fayette, Iowa Polar Bear Club took a plunge in the icy Volga River on a 28-degree-day last week.
He loved it. . . .

If you have any doubts about the appropriateness of a surprise, your ability to pull it off, or the editor's willingness to hide in the bushes with you, don't risk it. When in doubt, say it straight. You'll seldom offend or confuse a reader by being clear.

And in fact, addressing the reader directly can be a powerful approach, especially when you're writing how-to material. I use a *direct address lead* often in my service pieces for *Writer's Digest*. I tried to put the reader into the story from the beginning, for example, in a piece called "Seven steps to harnessing your creativity":

An idea strikes like summer lightning. That bit of dialogue you've been trying to write for days plays out like a movie in your mind. A brilliant article idea blossoms. A query letter seems to write itself.

Key words here are "you've" and "your." We're not talking about "writers" or even "a writer." We're talking about *you* and *your* writing. And the "you" is singular, not plural. We address readers, no matter how many of them we hope to attract, one at a time. Reading is, after all, a solitary encounter.

In a *Writer's Digest* article offering "12 ways to smash writer's block," I varied the direct address by including myself in the process:

For most of us, veteran and beginner alike, the hardest part about writing is getting started, getting beyond that often jarring, often numbing confrontation with the blank page or screen.

By using "us" instead of "you," I wanted to avoid giving the impression that I was in any way superior to the reader. We're all in it together.

For my article on "How to handle the press" for *Law and Order* magazine, I put the reader into this corner:

> A sensitive investigation is a tough job. But often the toughest part is the confrontation with a pack of reporters bent on yanking something "newsworthy" (i.e. "controversial") out of your mouth.
>
> Should you duck the reporters? Should you issue a terse "no comment"?

You should not, as I hope I displayed in 3,000 words outlining a better way to deal with members of the media.

And for *NurseWeek*, I posed another problem-solution lead:

> "We'd like you to edit the newsletter." Those words can strike terror into the heart of the most intrepid nurse.
>
> You know how much fun a newsletter can be — to read. . . . But your training is in health care, not journalism.

Direct address can work in contexts other than how-to, of course, as Marva York demonstrates in a stereotype-busting lead for the *Milwaukee Journal*:

> An alcoholic.
>
> The picture that comes to mind is of a wino on a park bench — old, unshaven, unkempt and stinking as he holds a flask wrapped in a paper sack to his lips.
>
> Now erase that picture.
>
> Paint over it the image of your 16-year-old son or daughter.

Powerful stuff, with a strong element of delayed revelation, but of a more direct and compelling nature than the trickery we explored earlier. York isn't referring to somebody else's cocker spaniel. She's challenging us to consider a social tragedy in personal, painful terms.

Sometimes the direct address sprouts a question mark, as with this powerfully involving lead by Tony Case in *Editor & Publisher*:

> How would you feel if your local newspaper published your yearly income for the whole community to see?

No theoretical discussion of public right to know here.

My double-question lead for an article in *Referee* magazine was more light-hearted:

> Are you out of shape? You? No way because you get plenty of exercise during your games, right? Wrong.

A *question lead* works only if the reader cares about the answer to the question. If a nurse has no call to edit a newsletter, and if a police officer never has to meet the press, they'll probably pass right by my articles. But if the how-to material isn't relevant to their needs, chances are they would have leapt over any sort of lead. The question spells out the potential relevance of the material, allowing the browser to make an informed decision.

For the question to work, it must be genuine as well as relevant. Avoid the cheap trick of the manipulative rhetorical question. We've learned to beware the phone call that begins with, "Do you want a good education for your child?" Of course I want a good education for my child. And as soon as I say so, I get the pitch for the encyclopedia, the home computer, the phonics course, or the test-preparation service.

We've learned to fend off such ingenuous queries. But an honest question, followed by honest answers or a sincere exploration of the possibilities, will engage us and even earn our gratitude.

The question need not speak directly to the reader's self-interest. But if it doesn't, it had better engage her curiosity. For a chapter heading in his autobiography, *Chuck Amuck,* master cartoonist Chuck Jones posed this question:

Why do animated cartoonists use animals?

Would you be upset if I didn't include Jones's answer? If so, it's a good question lead.

Cartoonists use animals, Jones asserts, because:

. . . it is easier and more believable to humanize animals than it is to humanize humans.

Elizabeth Kolbert leads her think piece for *The New York Times* with this wry poser:

How much longer can it be before there's a talk show devoted to the emotional trauma of appearing on a talk show?

And Margo Kaufman enlivens the travel section of the same newspaper with a question that surprises:

What is it about travel that turns people into raving cheapskates?

(Would it have been as much fun without the "raving"?)

Kolbert and Kaufman offer answers to their lighthearted queries. But the question need not be lighthearted, and you need not have an answer. You need only ask the question in good faith, as with this poignant lead from Bill Stokes for the *Milwaukee Journal*, datelined Arena, Wisconsin:

> Who would murder a nice old man in the peaceful valley several miles east of here?
>
> Who would beat Jim Paul on the head with something hard and blunt until it was impossible to make him presentable for his own funeral?
>
> Who would take him so violently in the 96th year of his life and deny him his ambition to live to be 100?

Good questions. Powerful lead. Stokes doesn't know the answers, but he clearly cares, and chances are you will, too.

The question may come in the form of multiple choice or a true-false test. But why would the reader want to take part in something as distasteful as a test? Ah, but these tests don't count against us. They merely challenge us to try out our knowledge, risk-free, before getting the answers and explanations.

Thomas Still makes the technique work for this article for the *Wisconsin State Journal*:

> Controlling the cost of Medicaid is easier than:
> A. Curing the common cold.
> B. Solving Rubik's cube.
> C. Finding a site for a new Madison Area Technical College campus.
> D. None of the above.

The city council had been embroiled in debate over siting the campus for months, so "C" was clearly a bad choice. Nothing easy about "A" or "B," either, so the answer was of course (D) "None of the above," meaning that controlling the cost of Medicaid is anything but easy.

I was hoping the reader would get the answers wrong in this test lead for *In Business*:

> True or false? 1) You probably can't qualify for an SBA (Small Business Administration) loan guarantee. 2) Even if you could qualify, applying to the SBA is about as easy as filling out the "simplified" tax forms. 3) Obtaining an SBA loan puts a blotch on your financial profile.

If I can get the reader leaning the wrong way, the answers will surprise her and might motivate her to read on.

> Okay, you can correct your own papers now.
> 1. Most likely false.

2. False.
3. Definitely false.

And we're off and running on a discussion of how you may indeed qualify for an SBA loan, despite your initial reservations.

Peter H. Lewis uses a variation on the quiz technique for the lead of one of his syndicated "Executive Computer" columns:

> First, a little quiz for all you executives: Everyone who uses a personal computer, raise one hand.
>
> Good.
>
> Now everyone who has ever felt like throwing the computer out the window, along with its software and manuals, raise two hands.
>
> I thought so.

With direct address, as with any method we might use to invite the reader to share our ideas and visions, the best technique is no technique, no gimmick, at all. The question, the startling statement, even the delayed revelation, must grow organically from the material. If we force it onto the material, it will simply draw attention to itself and perhaps repel rather than entice the reader.

And always, with this as with all aspects of our delicate and precious relationship with our reader, we must play absolutely fair, addressing the reader with genuine concern and respect.

CHAPTER ELEVEN

Getting Chummy — But Not Too — With Your Reader

Can we talk?

Some of the best leads don't seem like leads at all. It's more like two friends hunkered down over coffee, one friend, the writer, telling the other friend, the reader, an interesting story, something she has recently learned and is dying to tell someone. There's no condescension; the writer knows something the reader hasn't heard about yet, but that doesn't make the writer any smarter — only better informed on one specific topic.

The trick is to create the illusion of conversation — a relaxed cadence, comfortable diction, language in its shirtsleeves, as writer/teacher Bill Rivers called it. But it *is* an illusion. The writing must be better organized, less repetitious, more carefully crafted than conversation. After all, when you write, you don't have gestures and tone of voice to help you convey meaning, and you don't have a listener's raised eyebrow or glassy stare to let you know when you've strayed from clarity and relevance.

And you also need to be fanatical about accuracy, no matter how seemingly relaxed about diction — checking quotes, statistics and references as if your very reputation depended upon it — which, of course, it does. Once the error is out there in print, it's impossible to take back and very hard to correct, retractions somehow never gaining anything approaching the impact of the original error.

But all that effort and care mustn't show. The writing must seem effortless.

I started an article on vitamins with breakfast-table chat:

> The information on the side of a cereal box used to be pretty much limited to directions on how to send in for your Captain Midnight Secret Decoder Ring.
>
> But that was back in nutritionally-innocent times, when cereals could get away with calling themselves things like Sugar Pops and Sugar Jets, and Mom pushed bacon, eggs, whole milk, and other instruments of death on us as a "balanced diet."
>
> No more.

I then launched into a discussion of the nutritional analysis printed on the side of a box of Cracklin' Oat Bran.

Note the specific references to our shared culture — Captain Midnight, Sugar Pops, Sugar Jets. (I've really dated myself, haven't I?) The readers of my target magazine are my age and older, so I felt comfortable with these allusions. Note, too, the casual language ("Mom" rather than "Mother," "pushed" rather than "served," a reference to eggs and bacon as "instruments of death").

A few paragraphs down, I mentioned that my oat cereal also contains "a good slug" of various forms of sugar, and concluded, "Hey, vitamins are fine, but we don't want to get fanatical about it." This is beyond casual, lapsing into language with an attitude, somewhere between a chuckle and a sneer. I wanted to establish intimacy without getting pushy. (After all, it may have been our first "date" in print.)

Anne Raver used a personal, chatty approach for her article in *The New York Times* lamenting the passing of the Sears catalog.

> In 1958, I wanted a Tiny Tears doll more than anything else in the world. "Tiny Tears cries tears, wets, blows bubbles," the Sears catalogue said. "Squeeze her . . . see the big tears well up in her eyes. Hear her cry, too."

Raver maintained the personal tone throughout her discussion, coming back often to that Tiny Tears doll. Her conclusion was a sad farewell: "So long, sweet dreams, Sears catalog. And thank you for my Tiny Tears."

So how come the same fellow who is heartily endorsing Raver's approach here was admonishing you a few chapters ago to "get out of the way" and keep yourself out of the writing? How come it's okay, even commendable, for Raver, and an offense against nature for you?

I'm not sure I have a very satisfactory answer. First, I suppose, there's the matter of taste and personal preference. The Raver lead worked for me, easing me into a warm, nostalgic piece on an American institution.

I might not have even noticed her use of technique had I not been working on this book (and thus had my radar working full-time). But this personal lead, by another fine writer, seems to me to be self-conscious and forced:

> Karl Neumeier would like a paragraph in the newspaper to tell his old friends he's still alive at 97½.
> There you have it, Mr. Neumeier.

Clever? Certainly. Different? Absolutely. But I'm thinking about the writer (and her audacity, a trait I greatly admire in writers) rather than about Karl Neumeier, who has lots of stories to tell and really doesn't need a push start in the lead.

If personal references help to illustrate your theme and focus attention on your subject, you belong in the article. If such references and use of the perpendicular pronoun deflect attention from the subject, you're butting in where you don't belong. In this, as in all things, you must be the final judge.

I have two guidelines for judging when personal reference is appropriate.

1. Whenever you find yourself appearing in the rough draft of your article or chapter, question the relevance and effectiveness. If the guest shot survives your scrutiny, leave it in. If in doubt, pull it out and let the subject stand on its own.

2. If you plan on appearing, establish your presence early. If you wait too long to come out onstage, the effect may be about as smooth as if you suddenly sprang up in the middle of the second act of your play and started shouting "Here I am! I wrote this play!" You're bound to steal attention from the play you worked so hard to create.

Focusing on the trick, not the trickster

Any time you use language in an unusual or heightened way in the lead, you risk drawing attention to your magic instead of letting the reader enjoy the illusion. But you must take the occasional well-calculated risk to convert a browser into an involved reader.

Anna Quindlen, op/ed columnist for *The New York Times*, began her piece on what she calls "phonathon democracy" with this bit of wordplay:

> It's a good thing they invented the telephone. Otherwise some members of Congress might have to figure out how to work the touch-tone buttons on their consciences.
> The outbreak of phonathon democracy in our nation's capital

is a sorry exhibition of government in action.

Touch-tone consciences? A reach, perhaps, but a compact way to make a point.

Writing for *The Capital Times* (Madison, Wisconsin), Todd Moore risked a comparison to launch his analysis of local politics:

> Democrats are a lot like cats: When they're howling, it's tough to tell whether they're fighting or making love.

Do Quindlen and Moore have the right to take such liberties? Sure. Do you? You bet. "Writers can do anything they can get away with," Flannery O'Connor once noted. But then she added, "Unfortunately, they can't get away with very much." Ask not if it's permissible but rather if it's likely to work.

I received two press releases from the same writer on the same day. Both used wordplay in the lead. One worked for me, and the other didn't. You be the judge. Here's the first:

> Feminists needn't get ugly over beauty, for contrary to what-some of them believe, beauty can have a liberating effect on women.
>
> So says Linda Scott, an advertising professor at the University of Illinois. . . .

You could just as easily cut the mild play on words (getting ugly over beauty), leaving, "Contrary to what some feminists believe, beauty can have a liberating effect on women." But the initial banter cuts a potentially ponderous tone and invites me, a male, into what might have been threatening territory.

The second lead carries the play considerably further:

> Although their roots wrap around several standard disciplines, the scientists who study ancient soils—palaeopedologists—have no turf of their own, academically speaking.
>
> However, many of these "groundless" scientists will meet at the University of Illinois this month. . . .

Perhaps it's simply a matter of overkill. One pun might have been fun, but three in two sentences is two too many.

(Hint: If you feel the need to put quotation marks around a word that isn't a direct quotation, as with "groundless" in the example we just read, you've probably strayed out of bounds.)

Joe Beck used one pun and no quotation marks to create this winner for the *Wisconsin State Journal*:

Astrologer Neil Marbell went to court Friday looking to collect a fortune instead of telling one.

How to twist the tail of a cliché without getting scratched

Lead with a cliché? Never, on pain of death. But give that cliché a twist — trusting the reader to follow along — and you may have a terrific lead. AP writer Malcolm Carter took that tack for an article on fad diets:

Americans spend billions each year fighting fat with diets, pills, potions and gimmicks, yet heft springs eternal.

Get it? Heft for hope? Carter was counting on you to know the cliché without his having to explain it, since explanation would kill the effect. He hoped for a triple benefit — the resonance of the familiar phrase, the good feeling of having gotten the joke, and the surprise of the new usage.

Here's another twisted cliché, from Mark Davidson of the Newport News *Daily Press*:

You can lead a dog to water, but you can't let him drink — at least not in school.

Davidson's paper had run a photo of a dog named Jake slurping water from a fountain at Huntington Middle School, and parents had howled in protest. (Never mind that experts affirmed the old saw about a dog's mouth being cleaner than a person's.) Strong lead, but then Davidson takes the play on words too far, at least in my view:

Newport News school officials and police were dogged by complaints Thursday. . . .

Better to have let a sleeping cliché lie?

This AP story out of East Lansing, Michigan is out-front about trampling the trite:

Forget tiptoeing through the tulips. In Michigan State University's new world-class gardens, you can boogie by the begonias and rumba past the rhododendrons.

Sound and fury, signifying something — we hope

The conversational lead and the twisted cliché rely on trust between reader and writer. Let's relax the usual rules of order, they seem to imply, and share a laugh between friends. The writer trusts the reader to get the joke; the reader trusts the writer to manipulate language without manipulating truth or perspective.

We carry the trust a step further—and close the gap between reader and writer even more—when we develop an *allusion lead*, a reference, implied but not stated, to some aspect of our shared culture. Properly selected, the allusion illuminates the theme of the piece.

When a couple successfully sued a well-known airline after being bumped from a flight, an AP writer banked on our knowledge of the airline's advertising slogan:

> A retired judge and his wife complained that Delta wasn't ready when they were, and a jury awarded them $208,000 for being bumped from a flight—believed to be the largest award ever made to airline passengers denied their seats.

The allusion lead carries the same potential triple benefit, as the twisted cliché, but also contains a risk. If the reader doesn't get the reference ("Delta is ready when you are"), and if the lead doesn't make sense without this understanding, the reader will be confused and perhaps even annoyed.

By alluding to a television advertisement—the closest thing we have to a shared mythology—the writer was probably on pretty safe ground. Joanne Weintraub was equally secure in her assumption that we've all seen the sort of direct mail advertisement she alluded to in this *Milwaukee Journal* lead:

> MAJORIE STAUBER! YOU MAY ALREADY HAVE WON!
> HAROLD SHACKMAN! YOU MAY ALREADY HAVE WON!
> MILWAUKEE PUBLIC LIBRARY! YOU MAY ALREADY HAVE WON!
> But probably not.

As soon as we depart from the world of advertisements, however, the percentage of our readers who will recognize and appreciate our references may drop.

Fish are jumpin' and the profit is high.

—Annemarie Wess, alluding to "Summer time" ("and the livin' is easy") for her lead on the Annual Niagara County Fishing Derby for the Niagara (NY) *Gazette*.

This is a story about an old man and the sea—a really old man and the sea.

—Gordon Dillow, alluding to the Hemingway novel to introduce Tom Beston, age 101, to *Los Angeles Times* readers.

Every year the swallows return to Capistrano, the bulls run

**through Pamplona and the Bills lose the Super Bowl. Or so it
seems.**

— Lindsey Gruson, preparing *New York Times* readers for the
inevitable defeat of the Buffalo Bills by comparing it to a force of
nature and a ritual of humanity.

Again, it's a risk sometimes worth taking, but always remember that
you're taking a chance. And again, when in doubt, you can always simply say it straight. ("The Buffalo Bills are destined to lose the Super
Bowl every year. Or so it seems." Not nearly as much fun, but safer.)

Sometimes the allusion takes the form of *parody,* the lead rendered
in the language or format of the bit of culture being alluded to.

If you've read any of Mickey Spillane's tough-as-asphalt detective
novels, you'll no doubt get and appreciate this AP lead for a profile of
Spillane:

It had rained for two days. Now it was muggy. It was always
muggy when Mickey had some news to tell.

The brunette knew where to find him. She called him on the
hotel phone, as she tightened the belt on her gray trenchcoat.

"It's me," she whispered sweetly.

Great approach — for a few paragraphs. But the author wisely pulled
out of the parody and into the body of the article without belaboring
the parody — or the writer's cleverness. A little of this sort of thing may
go plenty far.

Terry Kelleher took a chance with this allusion lead for a Knight-
Ridder profile:

He's just an ordinary man, who desires nothing more than just
an ordinary chance to live exactly as he likes and do precisely
what he wants.

Have you identified Kelleher's subject? Chances are you're either
humming along to the lead, or you'll never crack the code.

An average man is he . . . who likes to live his life, free of strife,
doing whatever he thinks is best for him.

Who is this far-from-ordinary fellow? Actor Rex Harrison, at the
time seventy-four years old and about to have another go at the role of
Professor Henry Higgins in *My Fair Lady,* reprising a role for which
he had already sung "Just an Ordinary Man" 2,717 times. If you know
the song, you got the lead. If you don't, you might not want to read a
profile of the man who made the song famous anyway. But you would

have had to wade through the two paragraphs of song parody to know what you were rejecting.

I used the following lead to develop the theme that opening a new restaurant on Madison's State Street would be nearly impossible:

> How'd you like to try selling an assertiveness training course to TV Lenny?
>
> Or a set of Guy Lombardo records to Ben Sidran?
>
> Or a Bible to Anne Gaylor?
>
> No problem, you say?

Big problem, you say? Just who *are* these people? Unless you live in or near Madison, you won't know that "TV Lenny" is an aggressive merchandiser named Lenny Matioli, that Ben Sidran is a local jazz legend, or that Anne Gaylor is founder of the Freedom from Religion Society. And you also won't get my allusion lead, which worked for a local magazine but wouldn't work much past the city limits.

Local allusions are fine for the local audience. Medical reference is fine for *NurseWeek*. Whistle-blowing works in *Referee*. Match the reference to the reader, while still offering a surprise in the way you apply the reference.

Some allusions are audacious, not because the reader might not get them, but precisely because she will—but she might be offended. David O'Reilly took that chance for his Knight-Ridder story about a living creche scene in Philadelphia.

> And it came to pass in those days that a decree went out from the pastor of the Old First Reformed Church to have real cows and sheep and donkeys in the Christmas stable.
>
> So it was. And Christmases at the corner of Fourth and Race streets have not been the same since.

What could be more appropriate than echoing the Biblical language and structure of the Christmas story for a story about a Christmas celebration? But would some readers find the lead sacrilegious?

Apparently Joe Nathan Lamb didn't have any such qualms when he wrote this lead for *Publishers' Auxiliary*:

> In the beginning, God screwed up.
>
> He reached for clay and got Silly Putty, and then created not two, but three imperfect creatures: Adam, Eve, and the anonymous reporter, who lurked among the fig leaves taking notes for the expose.

Lamb asserted that reporters, in clinging to a false standard of objectivity, have failed in their obligation to question authority. And Lamb certainly practiced what he beseeched, developing a pseudo-Biblical tale that went over fine in *Publishers' Auxiliary* but wouldn't have gotten far in *Guideposts*.

Molly O'Neill was much more gentle in her religious allusion in the lead for her *New York Times* article on the decline of housekeeping:

> Dust bunnies under the couch. Cobwebs in the corners.
>
> A grimy shellac over the contents of kitchen cupboards.
>
> In a culture where cleanliness has long been equated with godliness, these telltale signs should be anathema. But rather than repenting with a vigorous spring cleaning, many Americans are changing creeds.

Again, it's a matter of letting the lead emerge from the material, and of matching the lead to the intended audience. The key is not "is it permissible?" but "is it effective for my audience?"

CHAPTER TWELVE

Why a Buffet Is Better for the Reader Than a Stew

*A*s is often the case with ambitious freelance writers, I had managed to pitch myself into a real bind.

It seemed like a great idea as I queried *Madison Magazine* to do a roundup piece on all the morning disc jockeys in the Madison radio market. I'd get to pursue one of my passions; *Madison Magazine* would get an informative, entertaining feature; I'd bank a nice check. Everybody would go home happy.

I had recently done an article on folks who work at night. Interviewing an all-night jock (actually, as I learned, they like to be called "personalities" now) had rekindled my love of radio. (If I weren't a writer, I might be a disc jockey.)

In particular, the drive-time morning DJs hold a fascination for me. Along with their afternoon commute-time counterparts, they're the make-and-break guys for their stations, the cleanup hitters. Stations put their strongest personalities on in the morning.

I jotted a few notes to myself, made a couple of phone calls, mostly to make sure the people I'd need to make the article work would talk to me for publication, and wrote what I hoped was a powerful and credible query letter, offering a compelling article.

Back came my query letter with editor Jim Selk's informal "Sure. When can I have it?" scrawled at the bottom. I was in business.

I conducted interviews at what most folks would consider to be rather obscene hours of the not-yet-morning, but I didn't mind that. I'm a morning person, and I like to see the world fill up with dawn light.

But a lot of those interviews, grabbed in between songs, commercials, headlines and the weather, came out rambling and disjointed. When I sat down to try to pull all the quotes and anecdotes together into a coherent piece, I faced a monster of an organizational problem. How could I weave all the individual threads into one tapestry, finding common elements among all the stories my sources had given me?

I recalled the wisdom of my friend Clarke Stallworth: "There are only two things a reader wants to know—'What do I get?' and 'How much is it going to cost me?'"

I knew I'd have to answer that first question by offering something of clear value in the first few sentences. But I didn't have advice or important information to offer. My readers could live quite nicely without reading my article about disc jockeys. I'd have to offer some combination of entertainment and insight into the human condition.

How hard would my reader work to get this insight? I figured I'd better make my offer in clear, simple language, to let the reader know that the cost in time and energy wouldn't be too steep.

"Keep the get high and the cost low," I heard Stallworth advising, "and you've got yourself a reader."

Hard-core radio fans would read the article for the subject alone (as long as I didn't take the life out of it). Fans of particular personalities might scan for information about their own favorite, might perhaps pause to read about other DJs as well. But they might also get tired of hunting.

And how to draw in the casual browser, looking for something diverting, perhaps a casual radio listener?

After thrashing around, trying out various leads (when it works well, I call this process "exploring the possibilities"), I realized I was asking the wrong question. I was like the Pringles potato chip people, who hit a block when they tried to figure out how to design a better potato chip bag. They finally found their solution to the problem of crumbling, stale chips when they asked the right question: "Who says it has to be a bag?" [They wound up putting their chips in the same sort of vacuum-sealed tube used to keep tennis balls fresh.]

I didn't need to answer the question "What's the best lead for this material?" I needed to ask a new question: "What's the best way to draw the reader into a series of related but diverse stories about disc jockeys?"

As soon as I asked the right question, I had my answer. I would create an umbrella lead, thematically connecting all the material, and inviting the reader to share the stories and indicating why those stories matter. Then I'd profile each personality in a separate vignette.

By changing the question, I wasn't taking an easy way out. Far from it. I now needed to create not one lead but nine, one for the article, one for each of the eight personalities I'd decided to include. I'd have to connect not once but nine times.

It was a risky strategy. Each vignette would provide an opportunity for the browser to decide to start reading. But each would also mean an interruption, a reminder that life is going on without her while she's reading something she doesn't have to read. So each break would also be an invitation to stop reading.

Editors call them "entry points"—and they like them

I've since learned that smart editors endorse the strategy I thought I was inventing. They call it creating "entry points" for the reader, and they've learned that it works. Instead of offering an all-or-nothing bowl of stew—eat it all or skip the whole thing—they offer a buffet. Eat just what you want and need.

Readers win, because the buffet is convenient and fits their need to make quick decisions. Editors (and thus the writers who contribute to their publications) win, because readers wind up reading more when given good, clear choices.

Dividing long articles into segments, each with its own headline and lead, as my material on DJs suggested, is just one way to build entry points into your writing. You can also break a long, complicated story into two or even three separate stories, as folks covering everything from the U.S. Supreme Court to the county council are doing. Or you can develop a story with sidebars, related pieces that can stand alone if the reader skips the main article.

I used a combination of these last two approaches recently by breaking a long profile of "writer's writer" Gary Provost into two primary stories, Provost on fiction and Provost on nonfiction, plus numerous sidebars. The sidebars included a short piece on finding markets, another on writing an effective query letter, and a breezy short on why we need to give our work strong titles, even though publishers and editors tend to change them.

Editors create additional entry points by developing active, informative captions for photos and other graphics, by breaking statistics out of paragraph form and into tabulated lists, by boxing off brief portions of text for emphasis, and by pulling important quotes out of the text and into large-type "pull-quotes" (also called "call-out quotes"), which are often run boldface and set off with bars top and bottom.

The result is a reader-friendly McJournalism, with material in nuggets, created not out of any misplaced notion that the reader is stupid and needs spoon-feeding, but out of awareness of the reader's severe time limitations and respect for her ability to choose what and how much she needs.

Back to the story at hand. I had determined that I would write not one but many leads. But where were all those leads to come from? I began pushing the keys, and my theme began emerging, without my willing or manipulating it, from all those conversations I'd had in cramped radio booths and station lobbies. If I had tried to explain the theme in one word, I might have picked "intimacy." Given a second word, I probably would have said "friendship."

The first three words appeared on my computer screen, setting the theme and tone for the article:

Our morning companions.

The words kept coming (in very short paragraphs. I guess I was going through a phase.)

They wake us up gently.
They keep us company over that first cup of coffee.
They share the ride to work and get the workday off to a bearable beginning.
And sometimes they become more than just a voice on the radio, a little talk between the tunes.
They become friends.

The lead was emerging from my research, yes, but also from a series of experiences I had had a long time ago. During my freshman year of college, many long years ago, I woke up every morning to the laughter of a man who called himself "Emperor Gene" on a San Francisco Top-40 rock station. "Emperor Gene" later became just plain Gene Nelson on another Bay Area station, and I switched stations with him.

I was thinking of Gene as I wrote the word "friends."

"They started young and worked cheap," I wrote, remembering my conversations over the last few weeks without referring to my notes. (I like to approach a rough draft like a closed-book test. I figure the things I remember without prompting are probably the most important elements for me in the story.)

They learned by doing. Many have been fired, some more than once.
They all love their work.

I had my lead and was ready to trot out my lineup of heavy hitters. I decided to let local radio legend Jim Mader bat first. He had been around for years, and his listeners were very loyal. Again, the lead welled up from my conversation with Mader and from my own experience. It came in the form of a quote that had surprised me during the interview and stayed with me afterwards.

> "It just takes a little discipline," according to WILV-FM's Jim Mader. Mader gets up at 4:30, but he rarely needs the alarm, waking 10 or 15 minutes earlier. "I can train anybody to do it," he says.

I'm that way, too, but I had thought I was the only one. Most of the folks I know say they have a terrible time getting up in the morning. I thought Mader's assertion would challenge the reader and perhaps evoke a "Oh, yeah?" response. (The reader doesn't have to agree with the lead, remember. She only needs to be engaged by it.)

I pursued my friend theme with another Mader quote, looking at the relationship from the other side:

> "You're not talking to a microphone," he says. "It isn't an audience. It's somebody.
>
> "They need me and I need them."

Again, I was drawing on experience. I had moved far from San Francisco and my morning friend, Gene Nelson, but on occasional trips to the Bay Area to visit my parents, I'd catch a few minutes of Gene in the morning. He changed stations and music formats again, but his act stayed essentially the same. He was still bright, still funny, still a friend. Listening to him was more than a quick laugh. He seemed to offer a double reassurance—that life had continuity, and that each day was not only bearable but downright laughable.

I attended a publishing conference at Stanford University for a week and tried to plan my morning so I could be near a radio for my favorite Nelson bit, "Uncle Gene reads from the funny papers," a few short quotes from the morning *Chronicle* news section, with a quick twist, a wry reflection, a gentle barb.

My "friendship" with this man I had never met was just beneath consciousness as I wrote my article. I put "Magic 98's" Pat ("Cleancut") O'Neill up next, leading with his quote about being "a radio geek" who always dreamed of performing on the air. His segment was quiet and reflective, to match his off-air personality.

Then came hard-charging Andy Witt of WTSO-AM country with an anecdote about a rogue woodchuck that once challenged Andy's right to do a remote out in the field behind the station.

"He charged and scared the bejesus out of me," Andy told me. I passed the vintage Witt-icism on to my readers, along with a lot of other shaggy remote stories, letting Andy fill the storyteller role so natural to him.

For Peter B (he didn't use his last name and didn't want it to appear in print), I began with a "highlight of my career" anecdote, about his successful campaign to get a short hunk of highway in town named after Elroy Hirsch, former star athlete and then athletic director of the University of Wisconsin-Madison. Peter B's pride at helping create "Crazylegs Lane" was clear.

> "After we broke down the remote," he recalls, "I walked up to both signs and just looked at them.
> I just stood back and looked at those signs."

I asked each DJ to name the major influences on his or her career and work. I was surprised and delighted when Peter B began to talk about a young jock he had listened to while coming up in Sacramento, California, a fellow named Gene Nelson. So my old friend Gene, whom I had never met, continued to ride with me through the article.

For my profile of Melanie Sommer, I played on a common misconception Melanie told me about early in the interview:

> A lot of people think Melanie Sommer and Bob Edwards are sitting shoulder to shoulder at the WHA microphones.
> But when public radio's Morning Edition comes on each weekday morning, Edwards is actually a thousand miles away in Washington, D.C., while Sommer handles the local newscasts and interview segments between network feeds.

Why do dedicated professionals like Sommer agree to keep impossible hours (except for people like Jim Mader) for low pay, with little job security? I let my next source explain:

> Two kinds of people go into radio, according to Paul Marszalek, morning man and music director for WMAD-FM. "The first kind is on an ego trip. They're just in it to get noticed. And the second kind," he says, "made a poor career decision. I'm one of those."

I saved my star for the next-to-last segment. J.D. Barber held forth on Top-40 format WZEE-FM, which at the time was enjoying enormous success (a twenty-five share of the market, unheard of for radio). Barber's story was reminiscent of O'Neill's (which is one reason why I separated them):

> As a kid, J.D. Barber listened to the radio "just about every night of the year."

His father was a cheesemaker, and the family lived outside Viroqua. "There wasn't a whole lot to do," Barber recalls.

". . . A career in radio just kind of evolved," he says.

Why not save the top-rated jock for last? Because I wanted to give the anchor position to Clyde Coffee (his real name was Downing, but he'd been Madison's morning cup of Coffee for years), my best how-I-got-started-in-the-business anecdote. I figured Clyde's story would reward the reader for staying with me for the whole piece, and it might pull in a few skimmers who had flipped to the end to see "how it comes out" before deciding whether to commit to reading the whole thing. I led Clyde's segment with this story:

When a landlady yelled at him to turn off the radio, Clyde Coffee knew he'd make it as a DJ.

He didn't have the radio on at the time.

That was just Coffee, sitting in his boardinghouse room in La Crosse, pursuing his dream.

"I always wanted to be in radio," Coffee says. "Oh, maybe when I was 10, I wanted to be a surgeon. Lucky for the human race I didn't do that."

Clyde's life was the archetypical radio success story. At the age of sixteen, he literally waded five miles through waist-deep snow to get to his job as technician for WOWO, Fort Wayne, Indiana, only to find that the DJ hadn't made it to work. "There wasn't anything else to do but to go on the air," Clyde told me. And so he did, and wound up with his own show.

Eight profiles. Eight offers in the leads. Eight chances to connect with the reader. And not one of them came from me. I listened to the stories and took the notes. I let the stories simmer in my subconscious, and when it came time to write, I let the stories emerge, let the subjects create the proper theme and set the appropriate tone for their own profile.

And all the while as I wrote, I remembered my on-air friend Gene Nelson, whom I had never met.

Just before Christmas after I finished the piece, I learned that Dad was dying of cancer, and I made several trips to California in the next eleven months to be with him and take care of him as best I could. After one visit, which turned out to be the next to last time I saw my father alive, I cried so hard as I tried to drive down the narrow Dogtown Road from Paradise Pines, I had to pull off the road for fear I'd crash the car. Almost in desperation, I turned on the radio. A rich, familiar voice filled the little rental car and stirred my heart. It was Gene Nelson, still on the air, still funny, still a friend. I drove on, my heart aching, my eyes tearing. My friend Gene Nelson kept me company and assured me that life had continuity and that this day, however much sorrow it bore, still somehow contained a laugh.

You know how you always think you're going to write to someone and tell them how much you appreciate something they did for you? But you never do, right? Or at least I rarely do. I never told my sixth-grade teacher, Fred Krause, for example, how he turned me around and helped me know what I could achieve in school. Or Bill Rivers, my college mentor, who wrote more criticism of my story than I wrote story, teaching me the craft that liberates the art of writing.

But somehow I found the grace to write a letter to Gene Nelson, to tell him how much his company had meant to me over the years, and how much he had done for me on one particular morning, when I was trying to find a way to let my heart say good-bye to my father.

Gene wrote a short note back to me. "You'll never know how much I appreciate your kindness," he said. But I think I do know, and I think the knowing came out when I sat down to write an article about the morning DJs in Madison, two thousand miles and many years later.

We write from our experience, our feelings. We bring all of ourselves to the writing. And we let the stories emerge, clear and unfettered, so they may tell themselves through us.

CHAPTER THIRTEEN

A Visit to the Lead Writer's Hall of Fame

You're an award-winning writer for a great metropolitan newspaper, and your editor has just handed you the biggest assignment of your life. You're to write a profile on—are you ready?—New York City, Gotham, the Big Apple, the City that Never Sleeps, the place where, if you can make it there, you can make it anywhere.

Paul Gapp had already won a Pulitzer Prize for distinguished criticism when he received this assignment from his editor at the *Chicago Tribune* in 1980. He went to New York, New York and immersed himself. Imagine the size of the clip file he must have developed. And Gapp didn't just hang out in the library and the newspaper morgue. He got out and wandered around, gathering stories and impressions to enliven the facts.

When it came time to stop gathering and start writing, he faced a problem every bit as immense as his topic—where to begin?

He could have retreated into statistics. After all, he had some incredible numbers to choose from, like the number of murders on an average NYC day (six) or the bank robberies (nine), or on the particular day in question the major explosions (one), fires (one) and impaired landings at Kennedy International (also one); or the amount of refuse collected each day, the number of books in the public library, the acres of forest cut down for a single edition of *The New York Times*, and on and on.

Gapp passed up the numbers option, deciding instead to focus on people. But he still faced a problem. If he opened the curtain on a stage filled with all seven million New Yorkers, the mob scene would have overwhelmed his audience. He chose to begin with a lone New Yorker, to ease us into a reflection on New Yorkers in general.

All those important and famous people to choose from — politicians, entertainers, athletes, eccentrics and street people, the one-of-a-kinders New York City seems never to run out of.

Gapp chose none of these, and none of the famous or fancy scenes the city afforded him. He opened his article, instead, with a humble scene and an anonymous protagonist:

> A young woman sits on a deafeningly noisy IRT subway train bound for the Bronx, and composes a poem on a pad of lined yellow paper.

She's writing a love poem (Gapp even quoted a few lines). In the midst of the noise and filth and confusion, she personifies what Gapp called "the art of survival" New Yorkers must master. Her soul somehow survives and even sings.

But even as the woman became a symbol, she remained an individual, perhaps an office worker, Gapp supposed, "probably on the homeward leg of a daily round trip." Still staying with the woman's point of view, Gapp did some more supposing, opening the scope of the article to encompass its huge subject:

> It is a good guess that she has never seen most of New York, for who can visit a thousand neighborhoods in a single lifetime? The place is simply too big, unthinkably complex, and full of hostile turf. Nobody "knows" this city. *Nobody.*

The woman gets off at the next stop. We never see her again.

Gapp was now ready to tackle the whole "dirty, glamorous, rotting, rich, ugly, glorious city." And I was ready to go with him, having been hooked into reading a long article on a subject of only passing interest to me. I don't regret the time I spent with Gapp's profile of New York City, and I've never forgotten the poet of the subway who enticed me to take the trip.

I consider Gapp's lead to be among the best I've ever read. The lesson Gapp teaches us works in any context. If you want to capture the general, focus on the specific. If you want to describe something huge and inanimate, begin with someone small and human.

The second lead in my Hall of Fame underscores the same point.

Polish Pope promotes absenteeism in Chicago

John Paul, the Polish pope, was due to say Mass in Chicago. Were Polish-Americans excited? Is the pope . . . well, you know how the line

goes. We needed something more than a traditional who/what/where/
when lead to convey the excitement, something better than:

> Pope John Paul is coming to Chicago to say Mass Friday. Polish-
> Americans are pretty excited about the whole thing. The Pope is
> Polish, you know. He's also Catholic, by the way.

I don't know how many people the reporter for the *Los Angeles
Times* (the lack of by-line for the piece is at least an outrage, if not a
sin) had to interview before finding Zofia Wysowski. Even if it were
hundreds, Zofia was well worth the quest. She provided the perfect
anecdote to reveal the importance of the pope's visit in personal, human
terms. The story began:

> Not once in the 28 years since Zofia Wysowski and her hus-
> band, Kazimierz, arrived in the United States with one suitcase,
> the clothes on their backs and $4 between them has she failed to
> show up for work as expected.

Despite sickness, three pregnancies, and the death of a child, Wysowski had compiled a perfect work record.

> But on Friday they will have to find someone to take her place
> on the midnight shift at the plastic shop. That is the day Pope
> John Paul will say mass in downtown Chicago. And that, to Mrs.
> Wysowski, is the one event worth missing work for.

The next paragraph opened out onto the nearly one million other
Polish-Americans in the Chicago area for whom the pope's visit constituted cause for celebration.

Big topic. Little lead. As with Gapp's New York City lead, this story
gets at the general by focusing on the particular, implies the universal
by describing the singular. A well-chosen, well-rendered anecdote has
that sort of power.

May I have this dance?

"This isn't rocket science," folks always tell you to let you know that
what you're dealing with ought to be a relatively simple matter. But
what if the topic *is* rocket science, or at least something a lot like and
every bit as difficult as rocket science? You're no rocket scientist, and
neither are your readers. How do you write about such weighty matters?

Award-winning science and medical writer Patrick Young liked to
say you must first find someone who speaks "Laymanese" (plain English). Then keep asking questions, Young advised, until you understand

what you're hearing. Only then, he insisted, should you start to take notes.

Victoria McGlothren of the *Wisconsin State Journal* faced this sort of challenge while covering a speech by a visiting *New York Times* science editor. Walter Sullivan's extraterrestrial talk to members of the Madison Civics Club ranged over the 150 billion stars in the galaxy and beyond, from the origins of life on earth to its possible demise a mere six billion years hence. How to make the cosmos comprehensible here and now? How to get the reader to journey to the stars?

McGlothren let Sullivan do it for her. She selected a quote that evoked an image and aroused curiosity without overwhelming us:

> "Think of a big, fat man trying to do the Viennese waltz with a skinny girl."

Got it. That's not so hard to imagine. But *why* are we imagining it? McGlothren told us right away.

> *New York Times* Science Editor Walter Sullivan drew upon this simple analogy to illustrate a more complex choreography: planets surrounding a single star, such as the sun, exert a gravitational pull that causes their star to move in an erratic manner similar to that of mismatched dance partners.

Sullivan, a fluent speaker of Laymanese, peppered his remarks with such folksy comparisons, likening the prospect of proving the existence of extraterrestrial life to trying to find your Aunt Isabelle at LaGuardia Airport. McGlothren had the wisdom to get out of the way and let Sullivan do his thing. And she had the grace to render his remarks in clear, simple English.

Little stories have become my biggest leads

Two anecdotes and a quote/image make up the top tier of my lead-writing Hall of Fame. And my three favorites among the leads I've written are all anecdotes. Little stories often make the biggest leads.

When I interviewed Doug Lyke, owner of a flourishing printing business and publisher of one of Wisconsin's finest weekly newspapers, I didn't have to work to get him to tell me the stories I'd need to create a good profile. Lyke was a genial storyteller who needed little prompting.

When it came time to write his profile for *Editor & Publisher*, I searched for the one story that would bridge the gap between the successful and respected businessman I had spoken with and the struggling young man who had brought his family to Wisconsin from Chicago years before to try to find a better way of life. I settled on this ironic juxtaposition of national and personal history:

> John Glenn was circling the earth.
> Doug Lyke was writing "executive wanted" ads for insertion in *The Wall Street Journal*.
> Lyke remembers staring out the window and thinking, "There must be more to life."

Lyke was working out of a three-person public relations shop in Chicago and living the suburban life. ("We all mowed our lawns at the same time," he told me.) But the commute had become a grind, and Lyke wanted more, or at least different. He wanted to be a newspaperman.

If I had concocted the contrast between Lyke's lawnmowing and an astronaut's soaring, I would have been forcing my judgment onto the material, and the lead would have seemed snide. But Lyke told the story on himself, revealing his personality while capturing the discontent that helped explain his later success.

I had almost used this quote for the lead: "I wanted to be a newspaperman." I loved the simplicity and power of the words, but I had used a similar quote to lead my *Editor & Publisher* profile of Mary and Pete Hollister ("Let's buy a newspaper.") And "newspaperman" is generic, whereas John Glenn is specific. Specific prevailed over generic.

I also considered several descriptive leads based on Lyke's adopted hometown, Ripon, Wisconsin, "Cookietown, U.S.A." and birthplace of the Republican Party. But the article was about the man, not the town, and the lead needed to establish the focus clearly and immediately.

I used another anecdote to open my profile of the controversial owner of a local radio station. This story came not from the subject himself but from one of his former employees, and the story was anything but flattering. I wrestled for a long time before making the choice, knowing that putting the story in the lead would give it tremendous emphasis and color the reader's perception of everything else in the article, including the subject's explanations and rebuttals. It was a powerful lead, but was it fair to my subject? I verified the story with other sources, gathered more information, and finally decided to go with an anecdote I felt to be representative of a strong majority of the opinions I had gathered. I'll change the names (and call letters) here to avoid hurting anybody.

Danny DJ remembers his last meeting with Armond Owner.

It came, DJ recalls, right after his Friday shift as morning man for WWWW-FM.

"I sat there in numbed silence," DJ says, "while they told me I was no longer a part of the future of the radio station." DJ then waited through "10 minutes of total silence," he says, while a secretary cut his final check.

He was one of five on-air personalities fired that day in what became known in local media circles as the "Christmas massacre."

I had a lot of other options for my lead. I could have gone with the controversy surrounding the man's replacement, as close to a "shock jock" as the local community would tolerate, or with the ongoing battle between the station owner and the local afternoon newspaper. I could have gone with the numbers; under aggressive new management, the station had made some healthy ratings gains. Although I generally avoid leading with history, the station had a rich heritage that could have made a good lead. But with the firing I had a hook that could immediately immerse the reader in the heart of the controversy surrounding my subject.

Both the Doug Lyke and the DJ leads presented themselves, the stories emerging naturally from interviews; I simply decided to use them. But I had to seek the third lead in this collection of my favorites; I found it in disaster for the subjects of the piece and in near surrender for me.

For one very long, very bad afternoon, I wasn't sure I even had a story, much less a lead. But my profile of Olaf and Peter Harken for *The Yacht* turned out to be among the pieces I'm proudest of.

Although the Harken brothers design and build their world-class boats in Pewaukee (near Milwaukee), Wisconsin, the magazine sent me all the way to Galveston Bay, Texas, to get the story of their attempt to set a speed record in a hybrid boat they called The Slingshot. But when I got there that evening, a clerk at a convenience store told me that the Harkens and their crew had smashed up the boat on a test run that afternoon. When I tried the phone numbers I'd been given, I realized that they were all daytime business numbers and thus quite useless to me. I couldn't even find my sources, let alone interview them.

No boat. No boatbuilders. No story. To make my joy complete, an arsonist was torching buildings in the area, and the locals were decidedly edgy around strangers.

I took myself on a walk, gave myself a pep talk, and began sleuthing. I couldn't afford to repay the folks at *The Yacht* for the plane ticket, so I figured I'd better get some sort of story.

I managed to find the ship's navigator, Mike Zuteck, who told me where the Harkens were likely to be in the morning. He then invited me to spend the night on his living room floor (I had neglected to secure a room), and I spent most of the night listening to members of the crew talk about sailing.

When I finally found the Harkens the next morning, their disaster turned into my good fortune; with no boat to sail, they had nothing but time and a need to talk about what had happened. I was, of course, quite willing to listen.

After this long, rambling "interview" in Texas, I arranged to visit the Harkens at their boatworks in Pewaukee for a second long session. I also talked to friends, associates, and other members of the boatbuilding and sailing communities. But I developed no clear notion as I was compiling all this material of how or where to begin my article. No snappy anecdote or succinct quote stepped forward, promising to do all the work of a good lead.

I kept coming back to that morning-after in Galveston, when two weary, hung-over sailors began to try to put together the pieces of their busted dream. I slowly realized that, no matter how hard it might be to make the article work, I had to begin it with that morning, because that's when the article really began for me. Here's what I came up with:

> The Harken brothers join the rest of Slingshot's crew at the City Cafe a little after nine. It's been a long night, and there's no reason to rush the morning.
>
> "Here we are, right in there with NASA," Peter Harken announces to Mike Zuteck, inventor of the "Zutelator" sail control system and author of the daily *Zuteck Slingshot Report*. "Did you tell 'em we went 45 minutes before we crashed?"
>
> They order the corned beef, eggs over, and coffee. Lots of coffee.
>
> "I hurt," Olaf Harken says. "I hurt real bad."
>
> It's his 46th birthday. When someone reminds him, he forces the kind of rueful grin made for a morning after.

Are you beginning to care about these guys? I hope so. That, of course, is at least half the battle in a profile and a major function of the lead. I was immensely pleased with the lead and the story that followed. But I did run into an organizational problem midway through the adventure, and I'll share the solution with you in chapter fifteen.

Heard any good lawyer jokes lately?

Since I've shared three of the leads I'm happiest with, it's only fair that I close with one of the leads from my personal Hall of Horrors, a case of writer indulgence coupling with editor excess to create a complete fiasco.

My assignment: Find out how local businesspeople feel about lawyers in general and lawyers' fees in particular. That's not as much fun as going to Galveston Bay to interview boatbuilders, but it's the kind of solid roundup piece that gets a lot of names into the magazine, entertains the reader, and perhaps even sheds a bit of light on an important issue.

I went into the research pretty sure of what I'd find; I expected people to tell me that lawyers' fees were way out of line. When they did, I figured I'd simply lay out a few of the most outrageous quotes, check the spelling of "gougers," and my lead would write itself.

Most everybody *did* tell me that lawyers charged too much—other people's lawyers, that is. Almost every source I contacted also told me that his or her lawyer was an exception to the rule, that their own attorneys charged reasonable rates and were always willing to provide extraordinary service in an emergency.

I guess that's why we actually have to research the articles before we write them, eh?

I had no choice but to abandon my preconceptions and create a lead that reflected the opinions I had uncovered. And I did write that lead. Honest I did:

> We love to bash lawyers. But we like our own lawyers just fine.

After quoting the financial officer of a local business explaining the "unusual" relationship with his attorney, I continued:

> This kind of adjustment is anything but unusual. In fact, where client and lawyer have established a long-term relationship, it seems to be the norm.

Not great literature, but an accurate, workable statement of what appeared to me to be the reality.

If only I had left it at that. But I didn't. I had to get cute. I had to tell a lawyer joke. And then another one. And I had to tell them at the top of the story, before the faithful, honest and maybe just a bit boring lead I had carefully crafted.

I had to ask, "What's brown and looks good on a lawyer?" (A Doberman.)

I had to ask, "What's the difference between a dead skunk in the road and a dead lawyer in the road?" (Skid marks in front of the skunk.)

But the editor didn't have to run the joke lead over a screen for emphasis. She didn't have to run a huge cartoon showing a lawyer grabbing a helpless client by the ankles and shaking all the money out of his pocket. She didn't have to run the headline "Are Your Legal Fees A Joke?" and the deck head "An itemized bill may keep them in line."

But I allowed — even invited — the editor to distort the intent of my article by using those rotten jokes above what should have been my lead.

I took my lumps. Sources and lawyer acquaintances called to complain. I got a few icy stares around town. I deserved them. But I hope I learned these lessons well:

* we must find the lead within the material rather than imposing it from without;
* the lead must reflect and reveal the theme or focus of the material;
* and most importantly, we must never sacrifice truth or clarity for the sake of cleverness.

Learn from my mistake, and you're likely to write many leads worth inclusion in your own Hall of Fame.

Part Two

INTERLUDE: BRIDGING

CHAPTER FOURTEEN

How to Get From the Lead to the Body and From the Body to the Conclusion

Congratulations. You've got her attention. You've lured the window shopper into your store. You've convinced the browser to become a reader, to put aside her life and devote her precious time to reading what you've written for her.

Now what?

Will you keep the promises you made in your lead? Did you make keepable promises?

Your lead should have at least begun to answer Clarke Stallworth's two key reader questions: "What do I get?" and "How much is it going to cost me?" The transitional bridge (which may be as brief as a word or as long as several paragraphs) must now begin to answer a third, equally important question: "So what?"

The reader wants to know how the subject applies to her, why she should care. If you don't tell her, you'll probably lose her.

Earlier we talked briefly about the after-dinner orator who spends the first few minutes of the speech babbling to settle himself down before launching into the real text of the talk. We compared this sort of throat-clearing to keeping your first two or three paragraphs of warm-up in your article or chapter instead of hitting the delete.

Now we encounter a second sort of speaker, who learned only half a lesson about capturing positive attention from the audience, the lesson about always starting with a joke.

"A funny thing happened to me on the way to the auditorium tonight," he might begin, or, "This conference puts me in mind of the

priest, the minister and the rabbi who were playing golf one day. . . . ''
Get the audience to laugh, some experts on public speaking say, and
they will be with you the rest of the way.

But *only* — and here's the second half of the lesson — if the joke relates
to the topic at hand, so the listener doesn't feel tricked when we reach
the inevitable, "But seriously, folks. . . ."

(The joke should also be funny, and the speaker should be able to
render it in a funny way, but that's another matter.)

If the joke is organic to the topic, the transition from the introduc-
tory joke to the body of the speech won't present a problem. If the joke
illuminates the theme of the speech, the speaker need only say, "And,
like that priest, minister, and rabbi, we face a serious obstacle . . ." If
the speech happens to be about ecumenical golfing, the speaker needs
no transition at all, and the listener need not even be aware that we've
moved from introduction to text.

In the same way, if your lead is a genuine invitation, an appropriate
promise, the transition or bridge should be natural, leading the reader
smoothly into the body, with no thought to turning back.

But if you impose a lead that doesn't really belong, or, worse, if you
try to trick the reader in the lead, you'll find yourself struggling to
come up with a plausible transition to make the trick work.

You might also trick yourself. If you create a witty, concise, memorable lead, you may become so dazzled by it, you don't really think about
whether this particular witty, concise, memorable lead belongs on top
of the particular piece you're writing. If so, your bridge can warn you.
If you've been carried away by your own cleverness, you'll have a devil
of a time developing a bridge to accommodate that dazzling lead.

The more clever the lead, the harder it will be to discard it. But
discard it you must. Remember, this is the crucial moment of decision.
Readers either quit here or stay with you the rest of the way. You need
an appropriate, functional lead.

Don't despair. Writing and then discarding that lead isn't a waste.
All writing is good exercise for the writer, and perhaps you needed to
write your way through this lead to get to the next one, the one that
works.

Let's test the footing on a few article bridges, judging the promise
of the lead for its appropriateness and seeing if an appropriate promise
leads naturally to a smooth bridge. (This paragraph is the bridge for
this chapter. Did you notice? We've finished the introduction and now
move into specific examples.)

I made this promise in my lead for an article called "12 ways to
smash writer's block" for *Writer's Digest:*

For most of us, veteran and beginner alike, the hardest part about writing is getting started, getting beyond that often jarring, often numbing confrontation with the blank page or screen.

Sometimes we hit writer's block, a solid wall of resistance to the task at hand. Other times, we encounter "writer's blank," ear-to-ear open spaces.

And yet, the real pros produce, whatever obstacles face them. What's their secret?

There's my lead, sixty-nine words to establish relationship ("most of us" writers), introduce the problem (writer's block and "writer's blank"), and make the implied promise (this article reveals the methods professional writers use to overcome these universal problems).

If the editor of *Writer's Digest* is correct in assuming that *WD* readers will be interested in those methods, the "So what?" question shouldn't be much of a factor here. And if my article will really reveal those methods, transition should be no problem. You be the judge:

> No secret, really. They combine motivation (no write, no job, no job, no eat) and discipline. And many of them have pet techniques for coaxing the words out of the mind and onto the page or screen.
>
> I'll offer 12 of these start-up techniques, which you can use to propel *your* writing.

And off we go, covering the sorts of jump-starting devices we explored earlier in this book.

You might think of the bridge or transition as the hinge that holds the door to the doorframe. It must be firmly attached to both. In my "writer's block" article, a single word, "secret," serves as the hinge by appearing in both elements.

For her profile of basketball coach and commentator Al McGuire for *50 Plus*, Cindy Lindstedt used a short, snappy quote lead and bridged crisply on "winning/winner":

> Al McGuire once noted, "If winning weren't important, nobody would keep score."
>
> McGuire has been a winner all his life.

Bob Rashid needed a more elaborate bridge for a more complicated lead, this direct appeal for reader empathy:

> Imagine you are eleven years old and you are leaving home for the first time. It's not a vacation you are going on, and behind the smiles of the adults around you, there is a sense of seriousness.

These adults, who you hardly know, are going to take you to another country. They say it won't be for very long. When you get there, you are going to have heart surgery.

By putting the key phrase at the end of the first paragraph, Rashid gave it particular power. Then he heightened the drama:

You can't bring your mother along with you. The adults say that they can help another child like yourself for the cost of that ticket. You have to go alone.
And something else: most of the adults don't speak the same language you do.

Interested? If so, you're in no mood for a "But seriously folks . . ." change of subject. You want to know who this little girl is, how she came to be in the situation Rashid has described for you, and how the drama relates to you ("So what?").
In other words, you're ready for the bridge:

This is the situation Eyra Karen Mendex Mendoza faced in March when she boarded Continental flight 775 with an American medical team in Managua, Nicaragua, and left for the United States. The medical team was in Nicaragua under the sponsorship of Healing the Children, a national, non-profit organization.

Rashid then provides a description of the subject: "Healing the Children is a national, nonprofit organization designed to give medical treatment to children who could not otherwise receive it." He could have lead with this functional but not especially gripping piece of information, but we wouldn't yet care. Instead, he wisely chose to begin with the particular, the human, before bridging crisply and naturally to the general information.

"It's a troublesome trade, and nobody asked us to take it up."

Quotes can prove especially tricky in bridging, probably because the temptation is so strong to cling to a powerful quote lead, even if the quote's connection to the theme is tenuous. Choose a quote that makes an appropriate promise, and you'll have little trouble creating a smooth transition.

Even with a quote lead that's both brilliant and apt, be sure to let the reader know right away why she's listening to it.

I often use quotes in my headlines and leads for writer profiles in *Creativity Connection*. In fact, I have to resist the temptation to lead with a quote for every profile. A quote lead can be a crutch, propping us up when we don't want to work hard to create a lead in our own words. But most of the writers I've been lucky enough to interview speak memorably about their craft. If I can't improve on their words, I don't try.

Here's the headline and lead for the piece I did for our keynote speaker at the 1991 Writers Institute in Madison:

> Fiction writing as a "benign neurosis" — Higgins
> "A writer is always a prisoner of his story," according to George V. Higgins.

Intriguing? I hope so. But now I need a bridge:

> If so, Higgins has been taken captive many times. He just finished his twenty-fourth novel.

I came back to the prisoner image near the end of the mini-profile, tying the piece back to the partial quote in the headline:

> "The characters show up. . . . Sometimes I wake up at 2 A.M., and one of those devils is talking to me. . . . It's very strange behavior . . . a benign neurosis. . . . It's a troublesome trade, and nobody asked us to take it up."

Answering Royko's "Sez who?" question

I hoped to encourage my writer/readers with this quote lead for a profile of a speaker at the 1992 Institute:

> "Good work will find a home," according to book editor Jody Rein.
> "We get paid on how well we say 'yes,' " not how well we say 'no.' "

I hadn't thought of an editor's job in those terms and found the perspective quite useful, so I led the piece with it.

The reader will now wonder who this Rein person is and what she knows about publishing. (Or, in the words of columnist Mike Royko, "Sez who?") My bridge must establish Rein's credentials without disrupting the flow of her thought:

> Rein has had an opportunity to say a lot of both. Until recently, she served as executive editor of the trade paperback division of Avon Books, one of the largest publishers in the country. . . . Before coming to Avon, Rein worked at Dell, where she acquired rights to bestsellers such as. . . .

Oh, *that* Jody Rein. I guess she might know a thing or two about publishing.

Along with credentials, we sometimes need to anchor a quote in specific time and place, rather than letting it float freely. That's another job for the transition. I led one author profile with:

> "Learning to write is learning who you are," according to Ben Logan, award-winning novelist and television writer.
>
> "The job is to get in touch with those undercurrents in yourself."

I needed to flesh out that "award-winning novelist and television writer" credential for any reader who didn't recognize Logan as the author of *The Land Remembers*. But first, I had to let the reader know where Logan was standing while he talked to us:

> He spoke at the spring Convocation of the Council for Wisconsin Writers.

And that's it for the bridge. We plunge right back into the essence of Logan's talk:

> We are a lot of different people, Logan said, and we must learn to draw on "all the beings inside us" when we write.

Leashing the shaggy dog story

Anecdotal leads can also provide bridging challenges. When we use a story lead to reveal the theme of the piece, we seldom begin at the beginning. An effective anecdote takes us to a point of particular tension or drama, regardless of its chronological place in the story. But to answer the "So what?" and "Sez who?" questions, we often have to ask the reader to do something readers usually hate to do—back up for the necessary background or antecedent action.

I faced the need for a "backup bridge" when I wrote a profile of Gary Milhollin, the law professor who tracks the worldwide spread of nuclear weapons. As you may remember, I began with Milhollin in action, well into his career as a "nuke stalker":

> Gary Milhollin faced the members of the Congressional Subcommittee on Technology and National Security last summer and, with characteristic directness and intensity, let them have it.
>
> U.S. forces in Saudi Arabia are facing their own technology, he told them. "If war comes . . . the West will be forced to bomb its own citizens to destroy its own exports."

I thought that scene so compelling, and so illustrative of Milhollin's crusade, I chose it for the lead, even though, chronologically, it's neither the first nor the latest event in the piece. So I had to create simple chronological bridges to maintain a smooth narrative flow.

The next paragraph began:

> A few weeks before, on July 29, 1990, Milhollin had warned in an article in *The New York Times* that Iraq posed a threat to world peace and that the United States was helping Iraq build long-range missiles and attain a nuclear capacity.
>
> Four days later, Iraq invaded Kuwait.
>
> Milhollin doesn't bother saying "I told you so." He's too busy tracking other threats worldwide.

I used the simplest of all chronological transitions to go back and pick up Milhollin's decision to abandon his teaching at the University of Wisconsin-Madison to become a nuke-tracker:

> Five years ago, Milhollin decided to try to stop the spread of nuclear arms to countries like Iraq by tearing down the wall of secrecy that protects such transactions.

(Key transitional elements: "Five years ago," "like Iraq" and "such transactions.")

I ended the discussion of Milhollin's career choice with what I still think is a great quote. Just who exactly assigned Milhollin the task of trying to save the world from nuclear destruction? " 'I appointed myself,' " Milhollin says."

And I seem to have appointed myself your advisor on leads, transitions and conclusions. In that self-appointed role, I'll devote the next chapter to that moment, deep within the body of the article or chapter, when you need a transition to get you out of a tight spot. I'll focus on an example of my own total failure to create such an internal transition.

And with that transitional tease, I hope I've enticed you into the next chapter.

CHAPTER FIFTEEN

Fighting Your Way Out of the Thicket

A few chapters back, I related my adventure in Galveston, Texas, with Olaf and Peter Harken, the world-class boatbuilders from Pewaukee, Wisconsin. As you'll recall, I decided to set the lead in a little cafe the morning after the wreck of the Slingshot. I allowed as how, in all modesty, I thought the lead constituted a pretty fine piece of writing.

Now I'll tell you the rest of the story, the part about how I got lost in the middle of the piece and almost couldn't find my way back out again.

After the anecdotal lead, I considered bridging to traditional exposition, weaving in quotes and anecdotes to keep the piece lively. But I decided to keep the piece in Galveston and stay with narration form, hoping to maintain drama and keep the reader happily involved.

The narrative form created the need for internal transitions to enable me to blend in necessary background and description without — excuse me — rocking the boat.

I waited, for example, for a good opportunity to work in a physical description of my subjects:

> In the early afternoon, Peter and Olaf pose for pictures on the crippled Slingshot. . . .
>
> "The price of fame," Olaf comments, favoring the camera with his rueful grin.
>
> "Infamy," Peter corrects.

> Both are solid six-footers. Olaf, the bigger of the two, is a bit heavier than he'd like to be just now. ("I saw a videotape of the Slingshot underway," he said later. "I was moving pretty good, but geez, I looked like a whale.")

The photograph session offered the pretext I needed for a paragraph of physical description (still letting the Harkens do the talking. I didn't want to get very far away from my charismatic subjects). The description in turn provided a natural hinge to a paragraph on their personal lives.

> Olaf is the family man, with a teacher/artist wife and three daughters back home in Pewaukee. Peter once got within bachelor-party distance of marriage before throwing the dog in the car and lighting out for Canada.

I let them relate the history of their boatbuilding business, which literally got started in a garage, using the theme of overcoming adversity as a bridge to a bit of family history as well:

> "I can't figure out to this day why we did it," Peter admits. "We thought of quitting so many times." He shoots his brother a quick grin. "Once we got going," he says, "we just kept telling ourselves, 'We gotta pull it through.' "
> The Harkens came by their ability to persevere naturally. Their grandfather owned three schooners that plied between Holland and Cuba. . . . Peter and Olaf were born in Indonesia and raised in the Philippines.

My piece was flowing nicely. My lead had enabled me to let the Harkens tell their good stories. Internal transitions came without my having to force them. All seemed to be well.

And then, like the Slingshot itself, my story crashed.

> Over bowls of the homemade chicken noodle soup at the City Cafe, Peter and Olaf decide it's time to get back to business. . . . The run for the record will have to wait. The Harkens are heading for home.

I headed for home with them. The rest of the information for the article came from a subsequent interview at their boatworks in Pewaukee. I couldn't work that material smoothly into a narrative set in Galveston—unless, of course, I cheated by creating "composite" quotes and pretending they all occurred on site in Texas. But we knew even before a recent *New Yorker* libel suit that misleading the reader in that way, or any other way, is neither fair nor right.

So I was stuck, a couple of thousand words into the piece and locked into a narrative structure. I couldn't abandon that structure without leaving the reader confused and possibly even angry.

Maybe things aren't as bad as all that, I told myself. I hadn't actually crashed, I reasoned. I'd just hit a lull. The wind had died down, and my sails had gone limp. I only needed to create a nice, strong transitional breeze.

I huffed and I puffed and I blew up a regular gale, trying out transitions. None worked. All seemed forced and contrived, bound to call attention to themselves by their clumsiness. My reader would hit the bump and suddenly remember that she really should start painting the kitchen or clipping the cat's claws, and I'd lose her.

These are the times that make us wonder why we didn't take up an easier profession, yes? Something like crowd control at English soccer matches.

Finally, I skipped two lines and typed "It is two weeks later." I really did that. In the great tradition of "Meanwhile, back at the ranch," I simply wiped the scene off the screen and started over.

I tried to create a hinge by alluding to the previous narrative, but it was more thong than metal latch. I don't know how firmly it holds Galveston to Pewaukee. You decide.

> It is two weeks later. Olaf sits amidst the creative chaos of his office in Pewaukee, sips coffee to soothe the sore throat that is probably a souvenir of Galveston, and tells the story of Peter and the Bear, or The Day the Russians Invaded Pewaukee.

With a fleeting glance back to Galveston (from whence the sore throat *may* have come), I pushed on. I could only hope that the transition wasn't too disruptive, and that my readers were by now enthralled with the Harkens and willing to endure a little bump to continue the journey with them.

Not all internal transitions create such problems. A good lead will often reveal or dictate its own story structure, establishing a smooth, natural flow. Good organization — telling the story in a way that makes inherent sense to the reader — eliminates the need for elaborate transitions.

My piece on Madison morning DJs, for example, needed very little twine to tie it together. If the lead worked to set the theme and draw the reader into the individual vignettes, I would have a framework for telling each story in turn. I had only to present good stories, in an order that maintained interest and built to a strong conclusion.

Still, I created hinges when I could. To get from Jim Mader to Pat O'Neill, for example, I built a bridge on luck and love.

I ended one segment with:

"I'm one of the lucky ones," he adds. "A lot of guys get up, and they don't want to go to work. I love my job."

and began the next:

Pat O'Neill's even luckier. He didn't have to wait until high school to find the work he loves.

They said it. I just arranged the material so that the two like elements would touch (sort of like playing dominoes, although I wouldn't want to press the analogy).

How much is too much?

The composer blends thousands of individual notes together. The audience hears a symphony.

We build our articles, chapters and books out of words, sentences, ideas, images. We move the elements around until we get good fit and flow. We smooth over the joints and polish to a high sheen. We don't want our reader to be aware of those component parts or of the effort we've made to blend the parts together into a unified whole.

We need transitions to smooth and blend, but we must be careful not to become too elaborate in creating these transitions. If we can add a bit of language to smooth the passage, without drawing attention to the fact that we've done so, well and good. But if instead the reader is made aware of the author or the artifice, we have hurt rather than helped.

I am often guilty of creating a more elaborate transition than the reader wants or needs.

My piece on Clark Wilkinson, the movie memorabilia collector, wound up as part of a much larger piece covering all the attractions in the Baraboo, Wisconsin area. So instead of a stand-alone lead for Wilkinson, I created this transition:

The [Al] Ringling [Theater], Circus World, and the Crane Foundation are the more visible attractions drawing visitors to Baraboo and offering residents unique resources for learning and enjoying. But there is a fourth treasure in Baraboo, one every bit as unique, educational, and enjoyable, although it is a bit harder to find. No marquee announces featured attractions. No canvas tent promises the greatest show on earth. No cranes trumpet the visitor's arrival.

Instead, a thin, bespectacled man greets visitors at the door and ushers them into the basement. . . .

In hindsight I think I made much more of a fuss than I needed to. How deeply could I have cut into this transition and still have moved the reader naturally into the next segment? Instead of all that recapping of the previous elements in the article, I could have simply begun with "There is a fourth treasure in Baraboo. . . ." I probably could have cut even deeper: "No marquee announces Baraboo's fourth treasure. . . ."

Helping the reader get ready to land

We need to talk about one more set of transitions before we reach the conclusion.

If you've been on a commercial airline recently, you know that a flight contains lots of transitions: checking in and saying good-bye to your baggage, passing through the metal detector, stampeding through the loading tube and onto the plane, buckling up and enjoying the confidence-building safety lecture ("in the event that we all wind up in the water, your seat cushion will serve as a flotation device . . ."). You know the routine.

Near the end of the flight, you feel the plane begin to lose altitude, initiating another important series of transitions. The flight attendant comes on the intercom to advise you to please take your seat and buckle your belt. You feel and hear the engines dethrottling. The landing gear descends with a disquieting bump. The attendant reads a list of connecting flights and gate numbers (but never, for some strange reason, *your* connecting flight and gate number). The pilot gives a weather report (in the same garbled foreign language with which he has awakened you several times during the flight to point out sights you could have seen had you been sitting on the other side of the plane). You're getting ready to land, waiting only for what must surely be the most ignored instruction in the English language: "Please remain seated until the plane comes to a full and complete stop."

You're ready. You know the flight's over.

The reader should know when your article or chapter is coming in for its landing. She may need a final transition to get her ready. The conclusion serves as that transition back into the world she left behind when she graciously agreed to make the flight with you.

We now turn our attention, then, to the fine art of finishing.

Part Three

THE ART OF FINISHING

CHAPTER SIXTEEN

Saving the (Second) Best for Last

My college biology teacher, Professor Donald Kennedy, was a brilliant lecturer. He had to be.

After all, he was trying to communicate the intricacies of a complex branch of scientific inquiry, packaged in tidy 50-minute parcels, to a huge audience of undergraduate students, many of whom were less than on-fire for the subject. (Some might have even signed on because biology sounded easier than physics or chemistry and still satisfied the lab science requirement. I couldn't have been the only one.)

Factor in the time (8 in the A.M.) and the setting (a cavernous, dimly lit auditorium), and you understand the challenge Professor Kennedy faced.

And yet, three times a week, he invariably kept most of us not only awake but alert, if not downright spellbound, as he described the genetic patterns of the fruit fly or the inner workings of the endocrine system.

Rather than simply relating the results of research, he described the often messy, sometimes chaotic process by which scientists reached their conclusions, including the false starts and blind alleys, the creative breakthroughs and leaps of faith that characterize science no less than any other creative endeavor.

He usually concluded with a brief preview of coming attractions ("Next time we'll take up the mating habits of the nematode") and ended precisely on time, a trait his audience especially appreciated.

But on more than one occasion, having built up the suspense as to the outcome of a particular line of inquiry, Professor Kennedy would look up, slowly close the notebook containing his lecture notes, look solemnly out at us, and say softly, "We don't really know." He would pick up his notebook and, without another word, exit, stage right.

I remember being thunderstruck (or as close to thunderstruck as a college undergraduate — required by statute to be blasé, if not downright nihilistic — could be). They don't know? Professor *Kennedy* doesn't know? How can this be? Doesn't Professor Kennedy know everything? And isn't science a static and certain body of lore?

I've forgotten much of my biology (I probably wouldn't recognize a heterozygote if I tripped over it). But I've never forgotten Professor Kennedy's indeterminate ending and its implication that biology is a living, evolving search for meaning, not a set of lessons to be learned.

Even a less dramatic conclusion is apt to be more memorable than anything from the middle of a presentation, simply because it's the last thing we hear. The same principle applies to written conclusions, which is one reason why we need to take as much care with how we end as with how we begin.

There's a second, equally important reason why conclusions are so important, one that applies uniquely to writing. The listener can't re-arrange a speech; she must listen to it in the order it's given. Not so the wily reader, especially the speed reader, who has learned to swoop and dive for meaning like a loon hunting fish. Such a speeder may read the lead and skip immediately to the conclusion, getting a capsule summary of the material, before deciding whether to read the whole piece.

For this sort of reader, the conclusion becomes a second lead, and lead plus conclusion combine to form a Big Lead. Thus, the conclusion becomes just as important as the lead as you try to compel the window shopper to come into your store.

So it makes sense to save your second best — or sometimes even your best — or last.

Here's an example. Patricia Leigh Brown wrote a long piece on "Street Architecture" for the Sunday *New York Times*, focusing on otherwise homeless people who fashion "homes" out of the city's left-overs. Brown and her editors wisely broke the material into sections, with strong subheads ("The architecture of despair," "There's no code for wiring shacks," "Ever so humble, but it's private") to guide the reader and to let the scanner pick and choose. Brown introduced us to a cast of interesting characters, primarily the street-level architects themselves and the sociologists who study them. And she came back to one of the strongest characters, a street builder from Brooklyn, to close the piece and reward the reader with this quote conclusion.

"Building it shaped my attitude. You realize you can do things for yourself. People who build for themselves have an interest in themselves. . . ."

Mr. Anderson knows what a home is. "A home," he said, "is the idea of who you are."

Brown didn't comment on or explain Anderson's statement. She didn't generalize or attempt to tell us "the meaning of it all." She simply, gracefully, let Anderson have the last, provocative word, and she let the reader reflect on its meaning for herself. That's a fine way to create a memorable conclusion and to suggest to the reader that she'll want to read the next article she encounters carrying the byline of Patricia Leigh Brown.

Writing for *The Chicago Tribune*, Janet Cawley also had the grace and wisdom to let her subject have the last word in her profile of journalist John Hockenberry. A former reporter for National Public Radio, Hockenberry was at the time of the profile about to take on a new role, as correspondent for ABC's videomagazine, *Day One*. Folks who had known Hockenberry only as a knowledgable voice on the radio were about to discover, as Cawley told us in the second paragraph, that Hockenberry the globetrotting journalist did all his reporting from the confines of a wheelchair.

Cawley drew no conclusions, expressed no emotions. If there was concluding or emoting to be done, she let Hockenberry do it, in this conclusion:

Minutes later, he grows pensive as he reflects on his life.

"I've been incredibly lucky. I get up every morning and go, 'God, don't complain, you idiot. There may be time for that later.' "

Anything more would be less.

Where is the writer in all this? Invisible, but everywhere present. Cawley captured the quote, after all, and recognized its worth. She saved it for the right time, giving it impact and power at the end of a long, excellent profile.

The author of a profile of Audrey Hepburn for *The New York Times* did the same thing—almost. But in the end, the urge to comment on a marvelous Hepburn closing quote overpowered restraint:

"I always love it when people write me letters and say, 'I was having a rotten time and I walked into a cinema and saw one of your movies and it made such a difference,' " she once said. She made a difference indeed.

Five innocent little words, "She made a difference indeed," restrained and justified by the text preceding them, but an intrusion nonetheless. They aren't "wrong." They don't ruin the piece or even the conclusion. But they do weaken both, robbing the reader of the right and privilege to evaluate for herself what she has read.

Read the conclusion without those last five words. Better? Do you need anything more?

Not all authorial evaluation is bad, of course. Consider the conclusion of the definitive and fascinating film biography, *Duke: The Life and Times of John Wayne*, by Donald Shepherd and Robert Slatzer.

In the book, the authors unraveled the mystery of the name. Wayne was born Marion *Robert* Morrison in Winterset, Iowa. But official studio biographies and even the Chamber of Commerce pamphlet from his hometown listed his true name as Marion *Michael* Morrison. Which one was right?

Neither, as the authors discovered with a great bit of sleuthing.

It turns out that Wayne/Morrison was indeed born Marion *Robert* Morrison, the given names coming from his grandfathers. But when he was four years old, his parents had a second son, whom they named Robert. Apparently feeling they had thus paid adequate homage to the maternal grandfather, they renamed young "Duke" (the nickname would come later, from local firemen), Marion *Mitchell* Morrison, the full name of the boy's paternal grandfather. So where did the Michael come from? From Wayne himself, who consistently lied about his name and took great pains to conceal the truth (apparently, the authors speculate, out of shame because his grandfather died in a mental institution).

The book moved on, through movies, wives and affairs, telling as good a yarn as any Wayne ever performed on the screen. In the end, the authors came back to the irony of the name:

> In a sense, the disposition of his remains is not important. Marion Mitchell Morrison lies in an unmarked grave by the sea, but to his fans the world over, John Wayne lives.

A big generalization, surely, and even a bit sentimental. But there's still room for the reader to maneuver in, to reflect on the nature of fame.

Conclusions about conclusions

What makes for a good conclusion? Why does one work, where another, following the same pattern or technique, fails? At the risk of drawing your conclusions for you, I offer three suggestions.

1. Never leave the reader turning the page, looking for the rest of

the story. Your conclusion should offer a satisfying sense of completion.

2. Like the revelation at the end of a good mystery story, the conclusion should offer a surprise (else why bother to read it?). And yet, once revealed, the conclusion should seem inevitable, the only way the piece could have properly ended.

3. The conclusion should leave the reader room to think and feel for herself.

Why bad things happen to great conclusions

There are two dangers in saving something wonderful for last.

First, no matter how good a job you've done of weaving your spell, no matter how unified and interesting your piece is, the reader may not make it all the way to the end. She may be called away or simply run out of time. The world rushes on. She never gets back to you. This is especially true with the more transitory and perishable print media — newsletters, newspapers, magazines. But many a bookmark never completes its march to the end of the book.

And secondly, the reader may not have a chance to read your conclusion because it isn't there to read. It's on the floor, or in the computer ether where all the deletes go, the victim of insensitive editing.

In the old days, most nonfiction for the popular media came in inverted pyramid form, remember, with all the important stuff crammed in at the top of the story, and information cascading in descending order of importance. A story didn't conclude; it just ended. Last was also least.

Editors liked that structure. If they needed to squeeze a 16-inch story into a 14-inch space, they could simply snip the last two inches.

Old habits die hard, it's said. Some editors still edit by Braille, without bothering to read the material they're chopping out, even for a story with a strong conclusion.

It happened to a reporter named Ron Seely, who writes human interest pieces for the *Wisconsin State Journal*. One piece profiled an ice fisherman named Joe Kowal, owner of the Polar Motel in Churchill, Manitoba. The story focused on Kowal's ability to handle sub-arctic cold. It would have been one of Seely's best, but an editor chopped off the anecdotal ending.

We follow Seely as he rides with Kowal into the inhuman cold of winter in Manitoba. Perhaps we pity Seely as he ventures outside the relative warmth of Kowal's pickup and into the 50-below temperatures of the tundra. If we've ever known true cold, we shudder as Seely reaches out to grab a steel ramp with an ungloved hand.

"My hand stuck to the thing like bubble gum to the bottom of a theater seat," Seely wrote. "I stood there for a second without the slightest idea what to do but painfully aware that my hand was freezing fast to the steel and aware, too, that if I pulled away I'd leave my palm on the ramp."

Thinking fast, Seely leaned over and breathed as hard as he could on his hand and "very slowly, pulled it away. It came, palm intact."

The story ended, rather abruptly, with those words.

But it shouldn't have. The story wasn't done yet. Seely had a topper. Having salvaged his hand and a bit of self-respect (Kowal hadn't seen him make an idiot of himself), Seely took out his camera to document the event. Forgetting the important lesson nature had just tried to teach him, he put the camera up to his face to aim and focus—and the camera of course stuck to his cheek.

I know the story because Seely told it to me. But most of his readers never got the full story or the fun.

After a brief look at some conclusions we know for sure won't work, we'll explore techniques for making your conclusions so good, so integral to their stories, even the most insensitive scissor-wielding, delete-punching editor should know enough to leave them alone.

Will these methods ensure that no editor will ever mutilate your writing and no reader ever misinterpret your meaning or skip your conclusion?

We don't really know.

CHAPTER SEVENTEEN

Three Conclusions Up With Which You Should Not End

"Never end a sentence with a preposition," English teachers have instructed since the discovery of grammar.

"This is the sort of English up with which I will not put," Winston Churchill is said to have retorted.

A noted television odyssey has survived season after season, attracting a considerable cult following, despite an ungrammatical introduction promising "to boldly go where no one has gone before." The crew of Star Trek's *Enterprise* splits an infinitive *and* dangles a preposition in one short sentence. So much for grammar.

Like many rules, the preposition proposition was made to be broken, or at least bent. Yes, letting a poor preposition dangle without an object to call its own can be confusing. But torturing the syntax to avoid one "crime" may lead to another, far worse, rendering—as Churchill wittily illustrated.

I say all this by way of warning. I'm about to suggest three ways you shouldn't end your articles or book chapters. In general, the tepid trio just won't produce the reaction you want from your reader (understanding, satisfaction, excitement, desire to encounter you again). In fact, they tend to produce the opposite reaction (confusion, disgruntlement, torpor, desire to cross the literary street when she sees you coming).

But—and here comes the caveat—like all generalizations (including, I suppose, the one I'm making now), the three I'm now proposing are prone to exception. If I say the conclusion is taboo, but you have a good reason to use it anyway — so long as that good reason has everything to do with what your words will do for the reader and nothing to do with your own vanity or ego-investment in a particular witty phrase you simply find too charming to abandon — then go for it. You have to make your own way.

But for lack of a compelling reason to the contrary, stay away from these.

1. *"And in conclusion . . ."* "Say what you're going to say, say it, and then say what you've said," speech coaches advise.

"And then," they should probably add, "sit down and shut up."

Good advice — for speeches. Since your spoken utterances exist only in air, you need to use repetition to emphasize key points and to make sure your audience notes them. Your words disappear the moment you speak them, unless, of course, they touch some responsive nerve in the listener, in which case, they, or the image or emotion they inspire, may linger for a lifetime.

But when you write, your words stay put. If the reader wants or needs to review them, she can take another peek. She can even clip them and haul them around with her, paste them in her scrapbook, laminate them and hang them on the wall. Repetition — the "say it, say it, and say it again" approach — is unnecessary and may be annoying or even insulting. If she doesn't want or need to reread, you shouldn't try to force her.

If you find yourself tempted to write "As we have seen" or any of its near relations, check yourself. Do you have anything new to add here? If not, why say it again?

If your conclusion begins with "In other words," stop, delete, go back and rewrite the original the way it ought to be.

Avoid the textbookish summary — "In conclusion, the three endings you should always avoid in your writing . . ." — even if you're writing a textbook. For emphasis, you might break those three key points out of their paragraphs and list them, with bullets, in a box, perhaps even over a tinted screen. The reader who wants or needs the reinforcement can read the list and clip it for future reference. The reader who doesn't want the reminder can skip it.

2. *"But one thing is certain . . ."* The more pressure you feel to come up with something extraordinary for your conclusion, the more likely you are to reach into the tool chest and pull out a cliché.

One especially creaky conclusion presents itself most often at the end of a television documentary. The earnest anchorperson has struggled to maintain a fair and objective demeanor throughout the hour-long investigation of nuclear waste or abortion rights or enforcement of Native American treaties. Now it's time to conclude, but how to do so without taking sides? ("Nuclear waste is pretty icky stuff. On the other hand . . .") So the anchor boldly straddles the center line, uttering something that sounds like a conclusion without really concluding anything at all:

> Nuclear waste continues to engage the best minds in our society. It's a subject on which good minds can sincerely disagree. But one thing's certain. The problem isn't likely to go away any time soon.

Yeah. Like for the next three billion years.

I don't mean to make light of the need for objectivity in the mass media. As writers, we often have the responsibility to present a balanced report on a sensitive subject, so the reader can weigh the arguments and come to her own conclusions. Such a presentation probably serves the Republic better, in fact, than any number of diatribes and polemics on the op/ed pages. But the "one thing's certain" pseudo conclusion doesn't clarify the issue. Instead, it pumps fog into the rhetorical landscape.

We could end, instead, with a strong conclusion from one of our sources, and in the next chapter, we'll explore the power of such a quote conclusion. But we must be careful about giving someone the last word when we're trying to balance two or more opinions.

For example, my article on long-distance telephone rates became a vigorous debate between phone company representatives and the outspoken head of the local Citizens' Utility Board, Kathleen O'Reilly. After trying to make sense of the issue and letting both sides have their swats at each other, I ended with what I felt to be a strong quote from O'Reilly:

> "We should be standing up proud for the gross receipts tax," she says. "If we had any leadership, we'd be going to other states and saying, 'Do what we did.' "

Much better, I thought then and still think now, to let the source have the last word than trying to come up with "the meaning of it all." But in doing so I gave O'Reilly a tremendous advantage. In any debate, whoever talks last talks best, because the last word has great impact and is more likely to be remembered.

So if you give one side the last word, you need to be aware of the advantage you've bestowed and perhaps compensate—by giving the other side the lead, for example, or a strong statement in the next-to-last paragraph.

3. *"Now it's time to bid farewell to our friend the aardvark . . ."*
You've maintained a friendly, conversational tone throughout the piece.
But you see the end coming and decide it's time to get serious. Suddenly
your writing takes on the ponderous, important tone of the narrator
in one of those "true life adventure" documentaries.

And your reader wonders what happened to that helpful, friendly
guide she has gladly been following.

Don't climb up behind the podium — or onto a high horse — for your
conclusion. If an informal tone has served you well for most of your
visit, don't abandon it for the good-byes at the door. Keep it light and
bright.

And, if you're among the first twenty-five to call . . .

To these three leaky dinghies, we might be tempted to add a fourth
boat to our list of ineffective conclusions. But we'd better not abandon
this ship too quickly.

Advertisers call it the "call to action." You've whipped the potential
consumer into a frenzy of desire for your hair restorer. Now you want
to clinch the sale. So you tell folks exactly what to do next.

"Send no money. Simply call this number. Operators are waiting to
take your order. Have your credit card handy."

To get you up out of your chair and over to that phone right now,
they may even add what's called a "sweetener."

"And, if you order now, we'll include Boxcar Slim's *50 Immortal
Love Ballads of the Pecos* absolutely free," which, as anyone who has
grown up in twentieth-century America knows, is much more free than
just "free."

"Order now, and the paring knife is yours to keep, with absolutely
no obligation to buy."

Why the rush? Because they know that if we really stop to ponder
the wisdom of ordering the hair restorer or the genuine simulated diamond ring, we're considerably less likely to do it. These are impulse
items. Gum is an impulse item, so we sell it in racks at the checkout
counter. A new car is not an impulse item (for most folks), so we don't
sell them in racks at the checkout counter.

If you've ever written a press release, you've probably created a
milder version of the call to action. After describing the wonderful
exhibit of Irish art soon to go on display at the local gallery, for example,
you end with some variation of the "For more information, please
call . . ." line.

It makes for a pretty tepid conclusion. It also leaves you vulnerable
if the same sort of editor who slashed Seely's anecdote snips your call

to action (thus leaving your reader all dressed up with nowhere to go).

But we'll probably continue to take that risk and tag our releases with the call-to-action line anyway, because the end is still the best place to put it.

We could have the best of both, a strong call to action and a sharp story conclusion, if we could get the editor to box the call to action, with telephone number and address, at the bottom of the piece, leaving us free to end the story with something fun.

Okay, wise guy. How *do* we get outta here?

If we aren't supposed to resort to the textbook conclusion, the "one thing's certain" cop-out, or the "true life narrator" high horse, how should we finish?

We'll spend the next five chapters exploring and enjoying excellent conclusions. As we do, we'll find that the best way to conclude is often the same way we began. We'll also note that the tone and style that carried us through the piece will take us the last few steps, too.

But for now, let's embrace a variation on the "less is more" theme. The lack of anything we might recognize as a conclusion is probably better than the three clunkers we've just discussed. Our material will often read better and have a stronger impact if we simply cut the last paragraph or two.

CHAPTER EIGHTEEN

The Return of the Magnificent Seven

*E*verything we've learned about starting will help us finish. If it works in your lead, it will work in your conclusion, too. The crisp quote, the compelling anecdote, the rich narrative — all the devices of effective lead writing — make for powerful conclusions. Come back to your original startling statement, which by now will no longer be a surprise, and top it. Enrich your original allusion with a second reference. Play out your play on words.

Prolific freelancer Dirk Johnson, who publishes often in *The New York Times*, began his piece on a kinder, gentler approach to the ancient art of breaking horses, by developing this scene in Greybull, Wyoming:

> At high noon in a crook of the Bighorn Mountains, the sorrel danced nervously inside the corral, as a lanky cowboy moved in to start breaking the colt — a practice as old as the Old West.

You can practically smell the mesquite. But what's new here? Read on.

> But this cowboy wore no spurs on his boots. He did not bark at the horse to show who was boss. He did not sneak around to throw a saddle on its back to climb aboard until it stopped bucking. Instead, he offered an outstretched hand, let the horse sniff it, and then gently stroked its neck and back.

Johnson then bridged on "a new generation of cowboys" who have forsaken tradition for a method "that shares more with the tenets of Zen philosophy than John Wayne bravado."

He built the body of the piece on the solid materials of quote, anecdote and description, including this great quote from new-age cowboy Dennis Reis: "I had to give myself a 'machoectomy.' "

And he saved a great cowboy quote for the very end, letting fourth-generation cowboy Tim Flitner have the last word on horse psychology:

> "They're just like people," the cowboy said. "In every herd of 15, you've got maybe two with some real talent, and the rest are just wishful thinkers."

We end with a smile and a surprise, wishing for more.

Dyan Zaslowsky saved not the second best but the best quote for the end of a long travel piece on Arkansas's Buffalo National River for *The New York Times*. When Zaslowsky noted the variant spelling of "Possum Trot," a hiking companion, a homegrown Arkansas native who "spoke in the soft, melodic accents" of the area, got the last word— and a gentle dig at know-it-all Yankees:

> "We don't have opossums down here," he said, lingering over the first o. "Just possums. Since you Northerners don't have any possums where y'all live, how come y'all the ones who get to decide how we have to spell the critters?"

Wisconsin wildlife writer Bryce Black began his outdoors profile with a quote from his subject, Sharon Phillips, about her prey, Brutus the Buck. (". . . I guess it was all because of him I started bow hunting.") He ended with an even better quote, letting Phillips supply the story's meaning:

> "Years ago, it was tough. A woman in the woods with a gun? They really looked at you cross-eyed. But I think that's changed now. . . . I think that's great. It makes me feel like I'm not a lost species."

What works for short nonfiction also works at book length.

As you'll recall, that marvelous exploration of the brain, *The 3-Pound Universe*, began with Saul, soon to become Paul, on the road to Damascus. Authors Judith Hooper and Dick Teresi then provided almost 400 pages of clearly rendered research into the brain. "So where are we?" the authors asked at the end of it all. But instead of trying to sum up this monumental subject by themselves, they turned to scientist Candace Pert for this closing quote:

> ". . . I don't feel an awe for the brain. I feel an awe for God. I

see in the brain all the beauty of the universe and its order—constant signs of God's presence. I'm learning that the brain obeys all the physical laws of the universe. It's not anything special. And yet it's the most special thing in the universe."

The mystery remains. I can almost hear Professor Kennedy murmur, "We don't really know."

Bob Edwards has surely learned the power of the telling quote during his tenure as anchor of National Public Radio's *Morning Edition*. He applied his knowledge of storytelling and strong endings to a subject most dear to him when he wrote his first (and so far only) book, *Fridays with Red: A Radio Friendship*, a reminiscence of his 12-year collaboration with baseball announcer and philosopher Red Barber. Red and "Colonel Bob" shared four minutes together each Friday morning, over 600 Friday mornings in all, talking of baseball, Abyssinian cats, camellias and other wonders.

When Barber died, letters of mourning and condolence poured in. Edwards says these letters compelled him to write the book.

He ended a chapter called "Moments" with a unique form of quote, a chunk of transcript from a November, 1991 broadcast, aired shortly after Florida State had lost a big game to Miami in Barber's hometown of Tallahassee.

Bob: Are hearts still heavy in Tallahassee this week?
Red: Well, I'll tell you something. I was around for the Ohio State-Notre Dame game in 1935, and the Bobby Thompson home run, and the Mickey Owen dropped third strike and the Chicago Bears' 73-0 win over the Redskins. And I saw the FSU-Miami one-point game, and you know what happened the next morning?
Bob: What?
Red: The sun rose right on time.

The rest of the page is blissfully blank. Edwards had the good sense to let Barber's wisdom linger without comment.

The well-chosen anecdote, sheltered from view until the last moment, can provide a compelling conclusion. Edwards knew that, too. He ended his chapter on "Brooklyn" with a brief story to illustrate Barber's effect as "the Voice" of the Brooklyn Dodgers. He introduced us to a Dodger fan named Steve Gorlick, who grew up in Los Angeles and moved to Brooklyn after Ebbets Field, home of "the Bums," had long since been torn down. And yet, Edwards related, on Friday mornings:

. . . he would time his morning run so that he would be at the site of Ebbets Field at 7:35 when I would be talking with Red on *Morning Edition*. For some time he thought he was standing near center field, but one of the locals eventually told him that he was at home plate. The important point is that Gorlick wanted to honor a time, a place and a man special to his neighbors. Red Barber had moved to a national stage, but he would always belong to Brooklyn.

A question seems a natural device to use in a lead, thus issuing the tacit promise that you'll in some way answer the question, or at least give it your best go, before you're finished. But could you also use a question as a conclusion? Mitchell Stephens, in his book, *A History of News: from the drum to the satellite*, seems to think so. After 300 pages of history with an attitude, he left us with a paradox to reflect on:

> The more profound, more sober side of our nature may never succeed in transforming news into an ideal vehicle for its concerns. Still, is there not something wonderfully human in this image of a future in which layer upon layer of finely worked circuitry is placed at the service of subject matter as unrefined, unruly and irrepressible as news?

Professor of English William Strunk, Jr., with prize pupil E.B. White, gave us a grammar book for the ages, *The Elements of Style*. They drew on metaphor and allusion to conclude their chapter on style, recalling Robert Louis Stevenson's rhyme about a cow "blown by all the winds that pass/ and wet with all the showers":

> And so must the young writer be. In our modern idiom, we would say that he must get wet all over. Mr. Stevenson, working in a plainer style, said it with felicity, and suddenly one cow, out of so many, received the gift of immortality. Like the steadfast writer, she is at home in the wind and the rain; and, thanks to one moment of felicity, she will live on and on and on.

The style is a bit elevated, almost ornate by modern standards ("said it with felicity . . . received the gift of immortality"). But this passage is consistent with the tone and diction, the implicit trust in the reader, displayed throughout the book. Two friendly, erudite guides lead us with patience and without a hint of condescension, the same two master writers who just a few sentences before had stated, "No one can write decently who is distrustful of the reader's intelligence."

Note please another salient feature about Strunk and White's conclusion; it *concludes*. It is consistent in style and tone with the rest of the book, and yet it rises to a gentle crescendo, ending the passage on a high note while allowing the implications to expand in the reader's mind (". . . on and on and on").

Another master writer on writing, William Zinsser, illustrated the same properties of excellent conclusions in his classic guide, *On Writing Well*. He ended his opening chapter on "Principles" with this wonderful reversal:

> Can such principles be taught? Maybe not.
> But most of them can be learned.

The introduction is clearly over. And yet, the words urge us on with the tacit promise that we can and will learn those principles.

Zinsser's chapter on "Words" ends with this admonition:

> Remember, then, that words are the only tools you will be given. Learn to use them with originality and care. Value them for their strength and their infinite diversity. And also remember: somebody out there is listening.

Again we have no doubt that the chapter has ended. And again, we're left with something to ponder. The paragraph extends the meaning of the chapter even as it brings it to an end.

Where Strunk and White were a bit distant, Zinsser got much closer, addressing us directly. Again, his tone and style are consistent with the rest of the discussion. He didn't put on a new voice or try to strain for extra importance.

Another of Zinsser's chapters ends with this compelling assertion:

> Writing is hard work. A clear sentence is no accident. Very few sentences come out right the first time, or even the third time. Remember this as a consolation in moments of despair. If you find that writing is hard, it's because it *is* hard. It's one of the hardest things that people do.

The chapter must end here, because there is simply nothing more that could be said on the subject. The conclusion rings with inevitability even as it avoids pomposity or false elevation.

A good conclusion, then, uses the same devices as those found in a strong lead, maintains the same relationship with the reader established throughout the piece, and comes to a forceful ending.

And it may do one thing more. The conclusion of a chapter isn't the end of the book, after all. While giving us a chance to pause, reflect and integrate, all good things for a reader to do, it also gives us a chance to find a bookmark, close the book, and return to earth, all potentially bad things for a reader to do, since there's always the chance we won't ever find our way back again.

So the conclusion of a chapter may in fact serve as an exhortation to read on, urging or easing us into the next chapter.

Science fiction master Ray Bradbury paused in his fiction spinning long enough to reveal the secrets of his craft in *Zen in the Art of Writing*. In his preface, he made it clear that, although he would be describing *his* life and *his* techniques, he wanted us to apply these lessons to *our* writing life.

In the conclusion to this preface (the end of the beginning?), he created a metaphor and gave it a sharp twist to carry us into the first chapter:

> Every morning I jump out of bed and step on a land mine. The land mine is me.
>
> After the explosion, I spend the rest of the day putting the pieces together.
>
> Now, it's your turn. Jump!

The introduction is over, but Bradbury was prodding us to turn the page and dive in. More great explosions ahead! You, too, can become a land mine.

This sense of conclusion as link from one chapter to the next is aptly illustrated in a photo essay book by Quinta Scott entitled *Route 66, The Highway and Its People*. In describing the great "mother road" that first connected Chicago to Santa Monica, California, Susan Croce Kelly's text links chapters into a nifty interstate of images and ideas.

The conclusion to an early chapter on paving, for example, firmly ends the chapter but just as firmly hooks it to the next, "Business and Ballyhoo":

> The paving of Route 66 was the second dream—after the fact of the highway itself—come true. And it was the beginning of another kind of dream, a personal one, for thousands of people in the states through which the highway ran, for these people saw nickels and dimes and dollars in every car that rolled down the pavement.

> Route 66 stretched in a great gray ribbon for over 2,000 miles, looping down from Chicago through Missouri and across Oklahoma, cutting a nick off of Kansas and slicing the top of Texas before stretching out for a straight run through New Mexico and Arizona and into the California desert and finally to the sea. You began in one place, and you ended up someplace very different.

This book on the Mother Road accomplishes the same sort of journey.

This sense of linear journey, with conclusion also serving as link, is important enough to merit a short chapter all its own. And so, compelled onward (I hope) by this linking conclusion, please turn the page and read on.

CHAPTER NINETEEN

"Tune In to the Next Thrill-Packed Episode"

*T*hey called them "cliff-hangers" for a good reason.

When I was a kid growing up in a small town in southern California (I'm old enough to have grown up in a time when there *were* small towns in southern California), I spent most of my time outdoors. But most Saturday afternoons found me, in the company of several hundred other squirming preadolescent males and a few brave girls, crammed into the Luther Burbank Elementary School auditorium for the Saturday movie matinee.

I loved the cartoons, of course, *real* cartoons, where more moved than just the characters' lower jaws. But most of all, I loved the serials — Flash Gordon, Captain Marvel, "The Mole Men Versus Superman," and scores of interchangeable westerns (some starring the young John Wayne, nee Marion Robert/Mitchell Morrison).

Each episode built to a dramatic climax. The helpless heroine plummeted over the cliff in a runaway buckboard. (Helpless heroines, no matter their other attainments, never seemed to know how to stop runaway buckboards by themselves.) Billy Batson, bound and gagged and thus unable to utter "Shazam!" to transform himself into world's mightiest mortal, plummeted over the cliff in a runaway panel truck. Flash Gordon, once again in the clutches of the diabolical Ming the Merciless, plummeted over some galactic cliff in a runaway spaceship.

"To be continued . . ." flashed across the screen. The mob of us in the audience, by now whipped into a glandular frenzy of suppressed violence, spilled out into the stark sunshine of late afternoon and onto the lawn outside the auditorium, to punch, pummel and pound one another, and later, in more reflective moments, to wonder how Hoppy, Captain Marvel or Flash was going to get out of the soup this time.

The conclusion of each episode thus lured us back for the next episode (as if we needed luring). It linked one episode to the next.

The new episode reprised the events bringing the hero to last week's mess. But it invariably added a new scene to the mix. We hadn't seen the heroine leap from the buckboard at the last minute, hadn't seen Billy Batson manage to work the gag off and utter the magic incantation, somehow hadn't noticed that Flash had revived in time to grab the joy stick and pull the spaceship (which in long shots looked very much like the tube a cigar might come in) out of its deadly plunge.

It was cheating, of course. But we didn't mind. We were kids, and we were there for the action, not for story continuity.

You can use the linking technique, too, to turn chapter and series conclusions into teasers, promoting the next chapter or article. You don't want the reader to find her bookmark, after all, and you do want readers to anticipate the next installment of your great stuff.

But you'd better not cheat. You're writing for busy adults, not for kids with endless Saturday afternoons to kill. You're writing for a discerning, sophisticated audience, not a howling pack of preteens who can barely hear the soundtrack for the first rush of hormones in their ears.

You'll use no tricks, then, no Billy Batson pulling off the gag while the camera conveniently turns away. Instead, you'll employ these solid linking techniques:

- End a chapter or article in a series with a dramatic and significant moment (without manipulating or contriving).
- Use quote, anecdote, description, or other strong conclusion technique.
- Craft language designed specifically to invite the reader to anticipate the next installment.

Erik Barnouw did all three in his fine history of television in America, *Tube of Plenty*. Barnouw concluded his chapter on television's infancy, "Toddler," for example, with the stock market crash and the bust year 1930, which stopped the development of television and left TV pioneer David Sarnoff apparently about to fall off a cliff. But Barnouw didn't leave us on this seemingly conclusive note, adding this teaser:

For [David] Sarnoff it was only a postponement. But his attention was also deflected to a new kind of crisis, one that threatened the very existence of RCA.

Sarnoff will somehow prevail ("only a postponement"), but he'll first encounter another crisis. What is it? Tune in to the next thrill-packed chapter. Reach for a bookmark? Never.

Radio survives and flourishes in the next chapter, bringing us to another peak:

> The end of World War I had precipitated the radio-broadcasting boom. The end of World War II held similar promise for television.

No hero going over the cliff here but instead the hint of a new hero riding onto the range.

Barnouw left us dangling at the end of the next chapter by hinting at greater things to come. He described the famous "I Love Lucy" episode in which Lucy Ricardo delivers a baby at the same time Lucille Ball in real life gives birth offscreen to Desiderio Alberto Arnaz IV (for the record, all 8½ pounds of him).

> The event found 68.8 percent of television sets tuned to *I Love Lucy* and was headline news even in competition with the Eisenhower inaugural, which came the following morning. The two events symbolized the moment. Amid the delirium, telecasters awaited the greatest of all booms.

Without that last sentence, it's a fine anecdotal conclusion, bringing the chapter to a definitive close. With the last line, it becomes a fine "tune in tomorrow" teaser, linking this chapter to the next and, Barnouw must have hoped, propelling the reader forward to find out about that "greatest of all booms."

The "Prime" chapter describing that boom ends in true cliff-hanger fashion, with America and Lyndon Johnson facing agonizing decisions regarding troop involvement in a far-off hunk of earth called Vietnam:

> Most television viewers did not yet know where Vietnam was; there were no network bureaus there. But they would learn.

Dealing with a somewhat more cerebral subject, but with a no less sure and compelling touch, Ronald W. Clark used chapter linkage to move us through his powerful biography of Albert Einstein, as enigmatic and charismatic a figure as any in the twentieth century.

Clark ended chapter seven, "A Jew in Berlin," for example, with this fine link:

> At the time, November, 1918, Einstein's naivete mattered lit-

tle. He was, within the comparatively small world of physicists, a creature of extraordinary power and imagination. Outside it, he was still unknown. This situation was to be dramatically altered within the year.

Clark chose the right place to end a chapter and summarize the significance of a period in Einstein's life. With the addition of the last sentence, he hinted at the importance of the next sequence of events.

In similar fashion, Clark closed the next chapter, "The Sensorium of God," with another linking conclusion. Einstein had:

> stretched out to touch untouchable things in a way that made him part magician and part messiah.
>
> That is, if the General Theory [of Relativity] were right. As Einstein, Born, and Wertheimer intervened with the students in Berlin in November, 1918, as the Empire went down to defeat, and de Sitter in Holland constructed his own blueprint of the universe, final plans were being made in Britain to discover whether this was so.

Note all the elements of a powerful conclusion: evocative, memorable language ("part magician and part messiah"), summation of significance ("if the General Theory were right"), and the cliff-hanger element (Is Einstein right? Tune in tomorrow, or better yet, tune in *right now*, by simply turning the page.)

These linkage conclusions propel us forward. But some journeys run in a circle rather than a straight line, and some prose achieves its power by returning in its conclusion to the same place it began in its lead.

Let's turn to an exploration of this different sort of word journey.

CHAPTER TWENTY

Ending Up Right Where You Began

We began our discussion of conclusions by observing that the sort of thing that works for leads — strong quotes, pointed anecdotes, poignant description, compelling wordplay — also works for conclusions. Now we push that notion one important step further by adding that a continuation of the *same* quote, anecdote, description or wordplay you used in the lead will often work beautifully in the conclusion. Your lead and conclusion can create a frame for the picture that is your article or chapter.

How's that for recycling?

Your prose becomes not a straight line but a circle. We travel the same distance in either case. But the straight line may leave us disoriented, unsure how to apply what we've learned, perhaps not even sure that the journey is over. The circle brings us home again, enlightened, entertained, perhaps even exhilarated, but back in familiar territory. At the end of the introduction to *The 3-Pound Universe*, Hooper and Teresi admitted that their explorations wouldn't solve the great mystery of mind, namely, how the brain becomes conscious of itself. "We still don't know whether 10^{11} wet cells make a soul," they wrote. "We find ourselves, like Dorothy after her adventures in Oz, back in Kansas where we started. It is, however, a *changed* Kansas."

Just so with the framed article or chapter. We're back where we began, but we have learned and grown from the journey. Home will never look the same.

The essence of the frame is twofold:

- You use the same technique and perhaps even the same material in both lead and conclusion, and
  - you reinforce a single theme or dominant impression in each.

Peter Lewis began one of his fine syndicated columns in the "Executive Computer" series by demonstrating the difficulties a user may endure when first trying to operate the particular technological wonder under review:

> Day One: This is being writings a worth it takes a while before the handed tiny red floor is footprint. Signed, Bite (poof!) Beers (poof!) been (poof!) I sits.

In the second paragraph, labeled "Day Two," the message, still somewhat garbled, emerges: "This is being written on an Apple Newton Message Pad." But problems remain: "It takes a while before the handwriting recognition is footprint (poof!) footprint (poof!) foolproof."

Lewis made his point; better yet, he made us feel the frustration. But if he made us feel much more of it, we might decide that the point isn't worth the pain. A little bit of this sort of thing is fun, but a lot becomes hard work. So Lewis wisely stopped with all the poofs and settled into his usual lucid prose for a crisp, readable discussion of the pros and cons of the Newton.

He returned to his lead technique only once, in the last paragraph:

> Apple deserves credit for simonizing the indignation (poof!) stimulating the imagination.

The reminder reinforces his theme and brings a smile of recognition. The journey is over, the circle completed.

Travel writer Joe LaPointe exhibited the same facility for drawing circles instead of lines with a piece for the Sunday *New York Times* on traveling to Montreal by train. He began with this simile:

> To choose to travel by train instead of by plane is like writing a letter instead of making a long-distance phone call. You have to want the slower pace, the scenery, the rhythm of wheel on rail.

The comparison works for me. I'm a member of that fast vanishing breed, the letter writer, and I love trains. I read on. I read on, please note, even though I have no plans to travel to Montreal, and no real hope of taking a train trip in the immediate future. I read on even though I'm in a hurry (always), anxious to get through the mammoth Sunday paper and on with my day. LaPointe created a true power lead.

He could have belabored the comparison. ("Instead of dialing yourself into a slim metal tube, you gently fold yourself into the train's envelope. . . .") But he didn't. In fact, he didn't refer to letters or telephones again. But in his conclusion, he drew a parallel simile, again relying on our sense of rhythm, to reinforce his theme:

> Train buffs are a little like connoisseurs of jazz or blues or country and western; there's a certain music in the sounds of wheels on rails and whistles in the night.

We've had a lovely trip, and now we're back at the station, safe and sound.

LaPointe's comparisons are gentle and, to me, unforced. In contrast, Stephen Whitty's language for an article on the Academy Awards for Knight-Ridder is raucous. But it's also thematically pointed and consistent: attitude in the lead, attitude in the conclusion. The piece begins:

> The Oscar is only gold-plated.
> And so are the Academy Awards.
> Like the statuette, the glittering annual ceremony coasts by on cheap sparkle and gilt. Underneath the veneer, it's made of baser stuff.
> But that's why we watch it.

After hammering away for several hundred often-slangy, usually breezy words, Whitty concluded that the awards ceremony:

> . . . will be as it always is — maddening, pathetic, sickening, absurd. And occasionally, mesmerizing. Like a car wreck, but with sequins.

We start with cheap sparkle and gilt. We end with sequins.

You can make a frame out of almost any materials. To illustrate the inevitable crashing disappointment we feel after watching the Super Bowl, *New York Times* commentator James R. Oestreich created his frame out of an allusion to a cultural icon, beginning his essay with this familiar fall scene:

> Call it the Charlie Brown complex. Every autumn, with infinitely resilient faith in the ultimate goodness of the human spirit, Charlie Brown throws his all into the kickoff, convinced that this time his sadistic playmate, Lucy Van Pelt, will not snatch the football away at the last minute. Suckered again, Charlie Brown.

And Super Bowl viewers are suckered again, because the game invariably fails to come close to matching the hype and the hope for it.

The return of Charlie Brown and Lucy in the conclusion signals the closing seconds of the fourth quarter. "Just maybe Dallas and Buffalo will muster a great game," Oestreich wrote. But then he made it clear that he didn't think so:

> . . . And oh, yes, Charlie Brown: give it another shot; Lucy won't pull the ball away this time; she *promises.*

It has been a quiet week . . .

Garrison Keillor is a storyteller, a mythmaker. He has written several bestselling books and numerous pieces for *The New Yorker, The New York Times,* and other prestigious publications. But those who love him best know him for his radio monologues — long, gentle tales about the people of the mythical hometown of Lake Wobegon, Minnesota, where (say it along with me if you're a Keillor fan) ". . . all the women are strong, the men are good-looking, and the children are way above average."

His opening never varies: "It has been a quiet week in Lake Wobegon, my hometown."

But underneath that quiet, the quiet-seeming people of the little Minnesota town have been living lives no less full of quiet desperation and occasional embarrassing bursts of passion than their brothers and sisters in the big city.

As he talks, Keillor clutches the microphone, closes his eyes, and begins to rock, breathing loudly through his nose to punctuate the pauses. The story unfolds, meanders, seems to get lost in digression on digression. But somehow, without map or compass or stars to guide him, Keillor always returns to the exact point where he began. We laugh, sometimes as much in recognition of and appreciation for the trick as for the gentle humor Keillor finds in the most humble aspects of the human condition.

You're probably not telling stories about Norwegian bachelor farmers, but you can use an anecdotal frame for some of your nonfiction.

Maureen Dowd began and ended her profile of radio commentator Rush Limbaugh for *The New York Times* with just such a thematic anecdote. As the piece opens, Dowd is having dinner with the famous commentator/author. A passing acquaintance, noting the company Limbaugh is keeping, remarks, "Well, Rush, that's got to be either a hooker or a reporter." And Rush, coiner of the term "feminazi" for radical feminist, is clearly embarrassed. The moment helps Dowd introduce a theme that emerges throughout the long profile: without a microphone and under all the bluster, Rush is a fairly shy fellow.

In the end, we return to that table at the 21 Club. The meal is over. The bill arrives. (Over $500 for dinner for two!) Limbaugh pays, and he and Dowd leave the restaurant. Limbaugh's chauffeur arrives on cue. And Limbaugh immediately tells him about the friend who made the crude crack in front of the female reporter. By returning to this anecdote, Dowd reinforced the point about Limbaugh's surprising show of sensitivity.

Ron Seely created a similar narrative frame for a profile of Superintendent of Schools Herbert Grover for the *Wisconsin State Journal*. The piece begins with Grover on his way to a hotel to address a gathering of high school principals.

> He hands over the car keys, says, "You can drive while I prepare my speech," and slumps into the passenger seat. He seems to fill the car.

Grover's nickname is "The Buffalo," partly because of his size, and partly because of his "head-down, full-gallop charge through life." A participant in the profile, Seely took us along as he tried to keep up with the galloping Grover throughout the evening. The profile ends when the evening ends, giving us closure and reinforcing the theme.

> Afterward, in the cold car in the parking lot, Grover is once again contemplative. With no question to prompt him, he says, suddenly, "Gotta make a difference, you know. Gotta light a candle. It's an eternal struggle."

We began with a quote in a car. We ended with a quote in the same car. The man who was preparing a speech off the cuff on his way to the presentation is still ad-libbing. It is, we have come to understand, his nature. Seely didn't have to tell us that; his narrative frame has shown us.

Quote/close quote

A few chapters back, I listed among the quote leads I've created this bit of wisdom from novelist/essayist George V. Higgins: "A writer is always a prisoner of his story."

I was holding out on you. There's more.

The focus for the piece is Higgins's contention that the writer discovers his plot as he writes. To reinforce that theme and to close as strongly as I began, I kept the rest of the opening quote for this conclusion:

> "I never know what I think until I see what I've written," he says. "I want to see how the story comes out. . . . It always comes out differently than I expect."

I also began my profile of National Book Award-winning writer Herbert Kubly with a quote—actually a quote of a quote, Kubly recalling his father often told him. "You'll give yourself a headache, filling it so full," Nick Kubly would say about his son's early love of reading, a penchant that earned him the nickname "Wunderlicher" ("odd child") among the people of New Glarus, Wisconsin, where Kubly grew up.

Of Swiss ancestry and an only son, young Kubly was expected to become a farmer like his father. When he announced at age thirteen that he wanted to be a writer instead, "relatives laughed at my joke," he said.

But his father didn't laugh.

We follow Herbert Kubly off the farm to New York City and then to Italy, Greece and Switzerland and back to the states for teaching stints in Illinois, New York and California. His journey ultimately leads him back to Wisconsin, and the profile returns to a recollection of his father. The closing quote completes the lead and extends the theme an important step:

> "My father was the bridge that made me possible. And he knew it. By his life, he was giving me permission to write."

I'm proud of that conclusion, not only because I'm moved by what Kubly said, but because I believed when I wrote it and still believe that adding another word to that ending would detract from its power.

I used a frame to extend the theme in my profile of Native American editor/entrepreneur Paul DeMain for *Editor & Publisher*. I led with this quote:

> "I don't think it's done out of racism," Paul DeMain said of what he sees as inaccurate reporting of Indian affairs by main-stream media. "It's done out of ignorance."

After a brief background paragraph, I let DeMain add to—but not yet finish—the thought:

> "Most of the time, the mainstream press ignores Indian affairs until there is controversy," he observed. "Meanwhile, our ath-letes, our educational programs, our people who have excelled go ignored."

After exposition of DeMain's career and philosophy, I returned to the issue of non-Indian coverage of Indian affairs, which, although bad, is getting a little better, according to DeMain. And then, in the last paragraph, I let DeMain tell us why the issue matters so much to him:

> "What I live for . . . is a dream or a vision, so Indian people

can chart their own future . . . so they don't have to clean the floors and chop the wood all the time."

The quote about mainstream ignorance struck me as a good potential lead the moment I heard DeMain say it. And when he shared his vision of his people, even though it was buried in the midst of a long series of interviews, I felt that I had my conclusion, unless something better came along to displace it. In my view, nothing did.

I constructed another frame to profile Bernie Little, owner of Miss Budweiser, at the time the fastest hydroplane in the world, for *The Yacht*. The profile begins with the observation that Little "eats antacids for breakfast on race days."

"I'm pretty uptight," he says. "I've got all these things going on in my head."

The piece follows Little through a race day, working in background and personal material. The story ends when the race ends, and it ends on the same theme, with a continuation of the quote and a brief observation:

. . . One race is over, but there's another to get ready for, more deals to make, more 'copters and yachts to buy and sell.

"I just gotta learn to slow down," he had said. But, as usual, he's in too much of a hurry to try.

Note the verb tense: "he *had* said." That's your tipoff that I've uncoupled that chunk of the quote from the portion I used in the lead, wrenching it out of time to save it for the end. We can move things out of sequence, of course; quotes, anecdotes and description are the threads from which we weave a coherent, unified pattern. But we must take the utmost care not to distort literal meaning or the speaker's intention when we take events out of chronological order.

But I didn't end with Little's quote. Did the conclusion need my comment? In good old hindsight, I wish I'd let Little have the last word.

If I had, I might have elevated this conclusion to the level of a true "snapper." What's a snapper? That's a conclusion that really packs a punch. The next chapter is full of them.

CHAPTER TWENTY-ONE

Putting Some Snap in Your Conclusion

You may have heard and perhaps read some of Paul Harvey's provocative "Rest of the Story" stories (now researched and scripted by Harvey's son, Paul, Jr.). By strategically withholding some key bit or bits of information, Harvey leads us through a profile of a famous character from history without revealing the person's identity until the end.

"And that man," he might intone, his voice full of profound pauses, "that humble soldier, who wound up walking home to Illinois after the Blackhawk Wars, that man was Abraham Lincoln.

"And now you know," he would conclude, his voice gathering momentum for that famous Paul Harvey chuckle, "the rest of the story."

The vignettes illustrate the art of telling an old story from a new angle, making the story new. And they also show the power a snapper ending can generate.

Engagement and surprise are the keys to the snapper ending. First we must get the reader involved in the story and its mystery. She must *care* how it turns out. The story must be intrinsically interesting, no matter whom we're talking about.

In the end, the revelation should surprise your reader. However, the story should be so well crafted, the clues so well placed, that the revelation seems inevitable. "Well, of course," the reader thinks. "I should have known." Otherwise, she may feel cheated, as when the mystery writer conceals an important clue, making it impossible to guess the identity of the murderer.

What if the reader does in fact correctly anticipate the "surprise" ending? ("I'll bet he's talking about Abraham Lincoln.") Need that ruin the effect? Not at all. She may feel proud of herself, and she'll read on for confirmation and affirmation. My brother and I used to get the same sort of pleasure, with an element of competition thrown in, watching the old *Twilight Zone* television shows and trying to see who could guess the surprise ending first.

Paul Harvey didn't invent the technique, of course — although he almost seems to have held the patent on it for years. An earlier radio practitioner of the art of the snapper, Fran Striker, used the same revelation show after show:

> "Who was that masked man, anyway?"
> "Why, don't you know? That was The Lone Ranger."
> We hear galloping hooves of the Ranger's great horse, Silver, and Faithful Indian Companion Tonto's Scout, galloping off to the strains of the William Tell Overture.
> "Hi ho, Silver, away!"

Walter Lanier Barber created snappers for some of the inspirational profiles in his book, *Walk in the Spirit*. You've not heard of the writer Walter Lanier Barber? Perhaps you know him as the sportscaster Red Barber or as the compatriot of "Colonel Bob" Edwards on Friday mornings on National Public Radio for twelve years.

Along with his pioneering work on radio and television, Barber wrote profiles of some of the people he encountered in sports — Branch Rickey, who broke baseball's color line by bringing Jackie Robinson up to play for the Brooklyn Dodgers; Iron Man Lou Gehrig, who set a record for consecutive games played only now being challenged by a fellow named Cal Ripken, Jr.; Bob Zuppke, "the Dutchman," who coached football great Red Grange in college.

Barber didn't try to conceal the identity of his subjects. Nor did he delay revealing the theme or focus of each piece. The profiles abound with strong quotes and anecdotes throughout. When Barber asked Zuppke what made Red Grange such a great player, for example, Zuppke replied, "What made Grange great — he brought with him," a quote that still stands alone for candor and humility. And in each profile Barber selected and organized the material to develop a theme.

His snapper ending, often in the form of a quote, extended the theme, underscored it, put it in bold face. You remember the snapper; you remember the theme.

In the profile on coach Zuppke, for example, Barber focused on Zuppke's ability to pull off a dramatic late-season upset. How did he turn sure defeat into unexpected victory?

"Keep your self-respect and you win," Zuppke said. "You may look like a failure and wind up a success."

Zuppke via Barber cited Vincent Van Gogh in the next to last paragraph. But Barber saved the most powerful quote for the last words:

> "But the greatest example of looking like a failure and yet winding up a success is Jesus on the cross."

Hard to top. Barber didn't try. He let the quote stand without comment.

Another snapper quote ends Barber's profile of the great Dodger catcher Roy Campanella, whose career was cut short when Campanella was paralyzed in a car accident. The next to last quote is powerful and inspirational: "I believe the Good Lord has spared me, has let me live for a purpose — for a reason."

The last quote is unexpected, memorable and succinct, and it extends the theme — a true snapper: *"I accept the chair."*

Barber saved another powerful quote/snapper to close his profile of star major league hitter George Sisler. How, Barber had asked, can you possibly concentrate on hitting, when someone is throwing a ball at you at horrifying velocity.

> "You watch the ball. You judge whether to hit it or not. That's all a successful batter can think about. *An afraid man can't hit.*"

Barber provided a meaningful measure of Gehrig's achievement with another snapper conclusion. He chronicled Gehrig's amazing career from the day he replaced a man named Wally Pipp, who took himself out of the lineup with a headache and never got back in, to Gehrig's death from amyotrophic lateral sclerosis (now known as "Lou Gehrig's disease"). Barber concluded with this stark, simple statement:

> June 2 he died, eighteen years and one day from Wally Pipp's headache.

Ernie Pyle's vignettes, like Barber's, often end with snappers. The stories, collected in book form as the classic *Home Country*, originally saw print as a series of dispatches for the Scripps-Howard newspaper chain, following Pyle on an odyssey around America. The stories hold up well in both formats, but we can see a subtle change in the way the snappers function when moved from stand-alone columns to book format.

One story, for example, finds Pyle out on the frigid predawn waters of San Francisco Bay with a group of crabbers. It is not, Pyle made it clear, an easy way to earn a living. The vignette ends:

We left the grounds at three o'clock, and it took two hours to twist and roll our way home. We had been at sea fourteen hours. On the way, Emile took off his boots and lay on the deck, steering with his foot. "How would you like to make your living this way?" he asked. Not I.

The story ends firmly. But after just two lines of white space, a new story begins:

Construction engineers are great fellows, and they are smart. They know all about stresses and strains. . . .

Out we go, with scarcely time to catch our breath, climbing up onto the Golden Gate Bridge, high over the very Bay we've just been setting our crab traps in. The two stories are thus linked by location and by a common theme—like crab fishing, working on the bridge is an extremely difficult and even frightening way to make a living.

Pyle used dialogue to create other snappers, as in this profile of champion poker player Mizzoo Townsend. The vignette ends with this exchange between Pyle and Townsend:

I said, "What was the biggest amount you ever played for?"
He chuckled and said, "Oh, not very big."
I said, "How long has it been since you played poker?"
He said, "Oh, quite a while."

A mundane exchange, made more so by the constant "I said/he said" business getting in the way of the words. But Pyle was simply setting us up for the snapper:

I said, "What did you do when you found people cheating on you?"
He said, "Oh, just quit playing."
Said his daughter-in-law, "He shoots 'em."

This snapper ending of Pyle's description of the Carlsbad Caverns provides a perplexing bit of trivia. The Park Rangers who lead tours of the caverns have been only partially successful, it seems, in keeping graffiti out of the area:

There wasn't a name on any of the rocks, and there was none in the men's washrooms. But in the women's, the Rangers said, there were ten thousand names. Figure that one out.

We can puzzle on it if we wish, as we might had we encountered the piece as a stand-alone column in the daily newspaper. Or we can plunge ahead to the next vignette in the book, a profile of one George Griggs, of Mesilla, New Mexico, and his encounter with Billy the Kid. Griggs actually saw the Kid only once when, as a little boy, Griggs was sent to the saloon for a bucket of beer. He entered the saloon and immediately recognized the famous killer. And what did Griggs do with this one brush with greatness in his life?

> . . . and little George Griggs turned and ran as fast as he could go.

Barber used snappers to intensify the inspiration he hoped readers would find in his profiles. Pyle was less reverent. And Norman Corwin used the snapper to create a sense of irony as he commented on a process that became the title of his book, *Trivializing America.*

He ended the chapter on the entertainment industry, for example, with this observation:

> There was no Pac-Man in the days of Monticello, no discos, no all-night movies, no DJ's, no Walkmans, no porno parlors, no drag racing, no *Saturday Night Live*, no divisional playoffs, no comic books, no horror pix, no Mrs. America beauty contests.

And then, having speared a representative of just about every type of diversion known to modern America, he added this twist: "On the other hand, there was time to read a book."

In wrapping up his chapter summarizing the development of radio, Corwin cited the resignation of CBS News President Fred Friendly as "one of the least proud hours of a network that had glittered in the Golden Age of Radio." A strong conclusion. Then Corwin added the snapper: "the shortest golden age in history."

He savaged the notion that television programmers simply give the public what it wants with this chapter-ending observation: "But the people have been conditioned to want what they want mainly by years of having gotten what they have gotten."

Remarkably, given the caustic tone throughout, Corwin ended on a positive note. The final snapper expresses if not assurance then at least hope that society might yet be salvaged by "a saving minority," comprised in part of Corwin's own readers, "the conscionable core, the humane marrow of America."

None of these statements are worthy of inscription on stone tables. But they gain power by coming at the end of a chapter, with white space beneath them providing emphasis and inviting reflection. What might have been wasted in the middle gathers power as a snapper ending.

True crime stories abound with snappers. They relate tales of violent adventure, after all, but usually with the mystery removed; the reader already knows how the story comes out. The writer must make the reader care, must create surprises and provide revelations along the way.

Mark Lemberger didn't plan to write a true crime book. But the unresolved murder of a relative led him to devote several years to researching and solving the riddle of who really killed "little Annie" Lemberger—the neighbor accused of the crime, or Annie's own father, Martin.

The details of the murder had been revived in the Madison, Wisconsin press periodically. When Lemberger wrote his *Crime of Magnitude: The Murder of Little Annie*, and Prairie Oak Press published it, the story received another thorough airing. So, many of the book's readers already knew at least the general outline of the story. Lemberger compelled them through the chronological narration with short chapters and frequent snappers.

The first episode, for example, describes Martin Lemberger searching (or pretending to search?) for his missing daughter. It ends with this misdirection snapper:

> Later that day, Martin, apparently clutching at straws, consulted a spiritualist who told him that not only was Annie alive, but she would come home to them on Saturday.

Wrong on both counts.

The snapper at the end of the next chapter increases the sense of urgency:

> Thursday afternoon Mayor Joseph Schubert promised a $200 reward to anyone who found Annie Lemberger.

Neither of these revelations is particularly striking. In the middle of a chapter, they would be lost among other details. But followed by the pause of a chapter ending—a very brief pause, in this case, since Lemberger simply skipped a few lines and began the next chapter on the same page—the news receives emphasis and heightened drama. Lemberger simply picked a good place in the narrative to pause.

A ne'er-do-well named John Johnson is pulled in as a suspect.

> He was questioned Saturday evening by Detective Pat Boyd, whom Johnson knew personally. The prisoner had little to say.

A nonrevelation, no news at all, given intensity as a chapter ending.

A Burns Agent named Boyer tells a local reporter he believes Johnson to be innocent. But . . .

Boyd kept his opinion to himself.

Another ominous nonrevelation. We plunge on. Johnson confesses, then recants.

His minimal confession had lasted just three hours.
For the rest of his life he maintained his innocence.

And so the tale unfolds, Lemberger skillfully marshaling his materials, building suspense for a crime procedural that happened eighty years before. The concluding chapters appropriately end with snappers to make the story resound in the reader's mind long after closing the book.

John A. Johnson's epitaph was spoken by his daughter many years after his death. When his name came up she crossed her arms, shook her head, and said, "He was no good."

The tale ends with a final quote, literally etched in stone. Annie's mother, Magdeline Lemberger, wins a libel suit against a magazine that repeated the conclusion that her husband, Martin, had killed their daughter. She shares the money with her four surviving children, then takes her share and commissions a new grave stone, with the name LEMBERGER carved in large letters on both sides, and underneath, this haunting inscription:

"Remember This"

Mark Lemberger could have found no better way to end his book, and I, this chapter.

CHAPTER TWENTY-TWO

Conclusion Hall of Fame

*H*ow better to end a book on leads and conclusions than with some of the best conclusions I've encountered in years of avid reading?

David McCullough is a master researcher, historian, teacher, and author of the massive biography, *Truman*. I tackled the tome because I wanted to know more about that feisty little failed haberdasher from Missouri, now being recognized as one of our finest presidents. I learned about Truman, all right, but I got a bonus—a fine lesson in how to end chapters (which begin well, too, by the way, with titles like "The Way of the Farmer," "The Moon, the Stars, and All the Planets," and, more predictably, "The Buck Stops Here" and "The Heat in the Kitchen").

McCullough used all the techniques we've explored, but he seemed especially drawn to the memorable quote conclusion. He ended the chapter titled "Try, Try Again," for example, with a double quote, the first from a Truman confidant and aide Ted Marks, remarking that Truman "strived for something and never let loose until he got there. . . ."

But McCullough easily topped that observation with one from Truman's cousin, Ethel Noland. "He didn't marry until he was 35," Noland recalled. "He didn't do anything early." But with politics, she concluded, "he struck his gait."

The selection of this quote is brilliant on three counts. First, the quote furthers the narrative by conveying specific information. Truman was a late-bloomer, in his mid-thirties before finding his life mate and his life's vocation. Second, McCullough let the credible source, a Truman relative, draw the conclusion rather than doing so himself. The conclusion has greater impact and carries greater credibility. And third, the phrase "struck his gait," a rural horsey idiom, creates the perfect image for a man who spent a lot of his boyhood following a horse and a plow around a field.

Years and chapters later, as McCullough prepared to tackle the years of the Truman presidency, he concluded the chapter on "Summer of Decision" with another quote — and created an eerie resonance. This quote came from Truman himself, in a letter to his mother, speaking of the "dizzy whirl" his life had become.

" 'Everyone had been going at a terrific gait,' he wrote, 'but I believe we are up with the parade now.' "

Again the horsey word to describe the pace of life, but now the metaphor is extended, the gait much faster. The horse is stretching out to catch up to the passing parade of history that will soon sweep Truman into the White House.

Fast forward eight years to the end of Truman's second term in office. McCullough needed the word or phrase or image that would enable us to understand and to feel what it must have meant for Harry Truman, the reluctant president, to be leaving office after seven years and nine months as the most powerful man in the world. McCullough didn't fetch a quote but rather a tiny scrap of detail, the sort of bit only a tireless and talented researcher could have uncovered and then recognized as gold and not just mere flecks of pyrites.

Truman is being driven by limousine from the Eisenhower inauguration and into private life. The burden of leading the United States and thus the free world has just been lifted from him; he is now Harry Truman, ex-president, once again a resident of Independence, Missouri.

Heading from the Capitol toward Georgetown, the limo carrying Truman reaches 7th and D Streets, where the driver stops for a red light. "It was," McCullough noted, "the first time that a car in which Truman was riding had had to stop for a traffic light since 1945."

The whole world of rank, privilege and importance is encapsulated into that one detail. The president doesn't have to stop for red lights. Truman is no longer president. Therefore, he's again subject to the same rules the rest of us must obey.

But that's not the end of Truman's day of transition or of the transitional chapter. McCullough took us to a farewell luncheon for the Trumans, full of tributes from old friends, senators and justices, members of the Cabinet, generals and ambassadors, all shaking Truman's hand and saying nice things about him. "He kept smiling," McCullough noted. Wife Bess looked "radiant."

The Trumans board the train, heading for home. The crowd on the platform sings "Auld Lang Syne" as the train pulls slowly away from the platform.

"It had been a long road from Independence to the White House," McCullough noted, "and now Truman was going home."

McCullough then let Truman have the last word, a bit of understated description from a journal entry made that night:

> "Crowd at Harper's Ferry . . . and it was reported to me at every stop all night long. Same way across Indiana and Illinois."

McCullough started his narrative in one small chunk of rural Missouri, but a mural depicting the life of a president soon needed a canvas large enough to encompass the world.

William Trogdon's *PrairyErth* is no less epic in its historic scope (and no less bulky—this is another *long* book!) But Trogdon started with one little chunk of midwestern land called Chase County, Kansas, and stayed there, finding the land and its people worthy of intensive study and the view from Chase County fully capable of yielding insights on the world.

You won't find the name Trogdon on the cover of *PrairyErth* (subtitled "a deep map"). Just as he had done for his first American portrait, *Blue Highways*, Trogdon wrote under his Native American name, William Least Heat-Moon. He had tried to find the voice and the rhythm for the first book through several failed versions of the manuscript. Only when he assumed his Indian name did the words begin to flow and the story properly unfold. So it was again William Least Heat-Moon who served as narrator.

Like McCullough, Least Heat-Moon often ended a chapter with a quotation or even a double quotation. To conclude the chapter entitled "Crossings," for example, Least Heat-Moon quoted a man from the town of Marion, explaining the possible derivation of a former name for the county: "We used to call it Chasem County. The story there was chase 'em, catch 'em, kick 'em."

Rough and tumble or not, Chase County, Kansas, looks "much the way visitors want rural western America to look." And how's that? Least Heat-Moon let a college student, a Pennsylvanian working on a ranch in the area, explain: "I can't believe this country. I can't believe it's still like this. I mean, it's so Americana."

More often, Least Heat-Moon let the natives of the area describe and define the sense of awe this quiet piece of earth can inspire. He ended a chapter on Saffordville, population five, with this quote from Edith McGregor: "Not everybody gets the chance to live like this."

The chapter on tiny Bazaar ends with "a friendly and loquacious woman" reading the diary of a previous resident and returning it to Least Heat-Moon with the simple reflection, "How far we've come from it all."

A chapter on Elmdale centers on the teenagers living in the county — and planning for their escape from a life they see as stifling. Least Heat-Moon let the kids themselves describe the frustration and the sense of limitation: "During rodeo, the adults block off Broadway and listen to music and drink," a young man named Dub relates, "the same thing they get after us for on a dead-end road."

The closing quote came from another time. "Days later, when I listened again to their words," Least Heat-Moon wrote,

> it seemed I heard a vision of a future Chase County very much like the one they knew, the difference being their absence from it. And I remembered a grammar school teacher here once telling me, *I wish we'd learn to love ourselves less and our children's future more.*

I won't try to thrust any of my own attempts at memorable and meaningful conclusions onto the same discussion with the work of Mc-Cullough and Least Heat-Moon. But I will reflect on the two endings that were probably the hardest to come by and which still mean the most to me of any I've written.

The first comes from my first commercially published book, *Freeing Your Creativity,* which Writer's Digest Books brought out in 1992.

Although I didn't know it, I'd been preparing to write my little book on creativity for many years, perhaps all my conscious life. I've reflected on the great gift and the mystery of the creative process, trained myself to use my own creativity more fully and joyfully, and made a vocation of sharing that exploration with college students and adult learners in workshops and conferences. I knew I had to write a book about what I had learned.

Writing is as much a means of discovery as a tool of communication. As I tried to write about the process and the power, I learned a great deal about what I knew and felt and had yet to learn. I also began to develop a sense of kinship and affection for the reader who might choose to share the journey with me. I knew nothing about this reader, of course; only after the book was published did I begin to get letters from people who found something of themselves in what I had written. But I had met them, some of them, in workshops and conferences around the country, and as I wrote, I wrote for them. They were the best kind of friends, the kind who would always listen to my theories as I worked them out on the keyboard. I felt connected to them.

As I neared the end of the manuscript, I realized that I didn't want this sense of connection to end. So the difficult task of writing a conclusion became even more difficult.

I began my epilogue with this admission:

> Just now, as I sat down to write to you for the final time . . . I had one final insight about the relationship between writer and reader.
>
> I realized how much I'll miss you.
>
> Writing this book has been like having an infinitely patient friend to talk to each day, about a subject I care for passionately.

"It's not an 'it' I'll miss," I realized. "It's a 'you,' the you I've been imagining as I wrote for all these months."

I dispensed some final observations about creativity. (It's amazing how addicting it can be to tell people how to live.) You can do it, I concluded, but it won't necessarily be easy. And then, after admonishing them to test everything I had written against their own observations and experiences, I realized that I really did have to stop typing and ship the manuscript to the publisher. So, lump in throat, I wrote:

> As we've noted so often during our journey together, you've got to do this your way.
>
> May your journey fill you with wonder.
>
> I hope you'll let me hear from you along the way, so that our conversation can continue.

I'm glad I wrote those final words, because many kind people have taken me at my word and written letters and notes, enriching me in the reading and them, I hope, in the writing. I hope they know that somebody on the other end cares.

I hope you know it, too, and that you'll write to me, % the University of Wisconsin Outreach, 610 Langdon St., Madison, Wisconsin 53703.

As difficult as this leave-taking conclusion turned out to be, it was easy compared to the final good-bye I found myself compelled to write at the end of a book I wrote that same year and published myself, with a press run of eight, under the imprint "Who the Hell Can Lick Us Press."

It is the story of my father's life. I wrote it for my brother and my nephews, for a cousin and his sons in California, for my father's people in New Jersey, and most of all, for my son, who had known and loved his "Grampa Coach" but didn't know much about his life. I hope the story will sustain and inspire him throughout his life.

Dad died of cancer in October of 1985. I was with him in the final days and hours of his life. Often after that I tried to write about that experience and about Dad's remarkable life and just couldn't do it. Anyone who has ever tried to put their deepest emotions into words will understand.

It took distance, several years and 2,000 miles worth, before I could begin to tell the story. I relied a lot on my memories. I drew on family albums and scrapbooks. I found rich resources I hadn't known existed—a diary Dad had kept while at the Naval Academy, a log he and Mom had filled out during a cross-country car trip in 1938. A ledger I had thought contained only notes Dad had made on fishing trips but which yielded a great deal of family history as well. I began corresponding with a cousin in New Jersey whom I had previously known only as a name on Christmas and birthday cards, and she gave me wonderful stories and details I couldn't have gotten anywhere else.

I ran into mysteries and dead ends. I found my grandmother's maiden name spelled four different ways on legal documents, one of several controversies I was ultimately unable to resolve. And yet, researching and writing the book were wonderful experiences. As I reconstructed Dad's life, I came to know not only the father who had raised me but also the vibrant young man he had been long before I existed. I felt purposeful and happy in the work.

Although I was eager to finish the project and put it into the hands of the next generation, I found myself reluctant to write the last chapter. It was more than a matter of completing an enjoyable task. When I finished the book, I would be saying good-bye to Dad in a way I hadn't yet done.

So writing this conclusion was especially difficult. I searched for the words and received instead an image, a vivid memory of an experience. That memory, of a hike in the Galatan Range of the Rocky Mountains in the Paradise Valley of Montana, became my conclusion.

> As I hiked the steep trail, I sensed that Dad was with me, inside me, seeing through my eyes the kind of country he loved best. On the way back down the mountain, I missed his presence and decided he had lingered by the lake.
>
> I've felt him with me often since. He's with me especially in the outdoors, and most surely as I walk in the woods . . . I ask him for strength in the hard times, and often I feel that he gives it to me. When making a difficult decision, I apply the test of his absolute integrity and honesty. He remains my guiding spirit. His

love strengthened and sustained me as I was growing, and it strengthens and sustains me now.

There are no words of gratitude adequate for this great gift of his life.

There was no more story to tell, and I had no words to try to extend the ones I had already written. The story ended there, because that's where it had to end.

I believe I've reached that point in this story as well.

INDEX